DRY AND SAVE

DRY AND SAVE

A complete guide
to food drying
at home . . . with recipes

Dora D. Flack

Woodbridge Press Publishing Company
Santa Barbara, California 93111

Published by

Woodbridge Press Publishing Company
Post Office Box 6189
Santa Barbara, California 93111

Published by arrangement with Bookcraft, Inc., Salt Lake City

Library of Congress Catalog Card Number: 77-72665
ISBN 0-912800-41-0

Published simultaneously in Canada
Printed in the United States of America

Affectionately dedicated to my mother,
for whom I, as a little girl, turned the drying fruit.

CONTENTS

Preface ix

1. Why Dry? 1

2. Methods of Drying 11

3. Pretreatment—Preservatives, Anti-
   Darkeners and Dips 23

4. Storing Dried Foods 29

5. Before You Start to Dry Food 33

6. Fruit and Vegetable Leather 37

7. Drying Fruit 49

8. Drying Vegetables and Herbs 79

9. Make Your Own Prepared Cereal 99

10. Miscellaneous Savers 101

    Bibliography 111

    Index to Charts and Recipes 113

    Subject Index 115

PREFACE

In 1972 two of my articles on making dried fruit leather appeared in magazines. This began an exciting new chapter in my life. As a result, I was asked to lecture and demonstrate extensively on the subject, which led to my book, *Fun with Fruit Preservation*. The lectures multiplied and so did the questions. I also learned from my more experienced listeners.

Fruit is only a part of the drying picture, and I had to go on to master its other phases, not only because of my own interest and curiosity, but because my listeners expected me to know.

Research and experimentation have been a way of life at our house for many years, since I am a co-author of *Wheat for Man, Why and How,* the popular whole wheat cookbook, as well as several other books. With six children to feed, stretching the food budget has been vital.

This book is the result of my search to fill our own family's nutritional needs and to be prepared for a time of emergency, our goal being to have a year's supply on hand.

Correspondence and lectures have convinced me that homemakers are eagerly grasping for information. The constant questions I receive have dictated the writing of a "take-me-by-the-hand-and-help-me" book. The home food-dehydrating field is burgeoning. More and more home dehydrators are flooding the market, with the consequent need for detailed assistance.

Constantly I am asked how to use the produce once it has been processed. Consequently, in addition to detailed instructions for preparation and preservation, many basic recipes are included, in the hope that you will build your own recipe file for using home-dried stores.

I have earnestly sought to make this book encompass all methods of drying, yet to keep it as simple as possible, so that even the new homemakers will have the confidence to persist.

Because every climate and home condition differs, it is impossible to answer every need. But perhaps with the help within these pages, you can find what applies best to your needs and locality.

Chapter 1
WHY DRY?

"Waste not, want not" is as true today as when the axiom was coined ages ago.

Drying is the oldest method of food preservation known to man—and is still the most economical.

From the time of the first realization that sun and wind removed moisture and preserved the food for later consumption, man has prepared food in time of harvest for nourishment during the unproductive months.

Through interpretation of the Egyptian pharaoh's dream, Joseph was able to direct the storage of food during the seven years of plenty for the seven years of famine. Only corn is mentioned specifically in the Genesis account, but surely Israelite and Egyptian survival was dependent upon more than grain. Their stored supplies must have also included dried fruits and vegetables common to the locale, because the skill was practiced before that time.

Ancient explorers depended on dried foods on their long voyages and treks. Some of us recall the drying food hung from rafters or over a woodstove or fireplace at Grandmother's house. This was a common sight in Europe. Grandmother hung drying foods in the attic or a back bedroom as well.

As knowledge of bacteriology grew and new food preservation methods were developed, we moved away from drying, terming it old-fashioned. Today modern refrigeration and canning methods, as well as speedy transportation, bring fresh foods to our tables from great distances the year around.

The human body requires balanced nutrition. If fresh fruits and vegetables are not immediately available, then dried, canned, or frozen products are necessary.

In war-torn Europe following World War II, malnutrition was probably due more to the lack of fruits than to any other one thing. A group of generous neighbors in Utah were preparing shipments of food and clothing for war-ravaged survivors in a specific area in Germany which had been severely bombed. (Anyone who remembers World War II recalls the impoverished conditions of those nations.) These good neighbors accumulated clothes, bedding and food to share.

One woman in that neighborhood was known for her frugality, which actually bordered on stinginess. She wasn't about to share her bounties, but neither would her conscience allow her to ignore the mercy project.

So she gave a cloth sack of dried fruit which, for several years, she had stored under haphazard conditions. The fruit was black and unappetizing, and her neighbors reluctantly included it in the shipment. When these neighbors received written thanks from those grateful German recipients, the only item which was specifically mentioned—and with superlatives—was the ugly dried fruit!

Of course, European orchards had been bombed out, and fruit trees require several years of growth before producing a crop. Those German people were starved for fruit, no matter what its condition.

If supermarkets in America were to close their doors due to shortages, transportation strikes, or other calamities, many people would simply starve to death, because too few provisions have been stored in homes.

But why dry?

Economy in Storage Space

When there is an abundance of fruit, vegetables, and herbs, available at little or no cost in the home garden or purchased directly from the farmer at harvest time at substantial savings, there is a limit to the amount that can be preserved in "wet pack." Dried foods take one-tenth or less the storage space of wet pack. For example, half a bushel of apricots dried can be stored in two quart jars and one pint jar.

Other Economies

1. The fluctuating price of sugar dictates cutting its consumption. Also more and more researchers are discovering the detrimental effects of excessive sugar on the human body.

2. Bottles and lids have been in short supply some seasons. As if scarcity were not problem enough, homemakers have found that many of the lids would not seal, resulting in waste and frustration.

3. Having a home garden and a few fruit trees can supply a large proportion of a family's produce needs. The trouble is, harvest brings too much all at once. Most homemakers put their surplus in bottles, but when the bottles and shelves are filled, what do you do? You can't give the produce away, because everyone else on the block is trying to give his to you.

4. There's the problem of having not enough vegetables of one variety at one picking to fill a pressure cooker—just small quantities which certainly can't be canned at the same time because of a variance of

Why Dry?

specified cooking time. Those small amounts can be dried and stored for future use instead of being wasted.

5. Energy is saved by drying, even if a dehydrator is used. An electric dehydrator should not use any more power than a television set. An electric oven at the lowest setting uses very little electricity (about five cents per hour—90 percent lower than when it operates at medium or high heat, which is certainly an economy over buying dried foods in the market). In addition, you have probably salvaged surplus food that would have been wasted. The pilot light of a gas oven is usually sufficient for drying. Of course, you must keep the oven door ajar for circulation.

6. Rather than waste onions that are losing their firmness, dry them for use in soups and stews. Of course, firm produce is best, but we're talking about saving—food as well as money. A 7-oz. jar of onion flakes costs over a dollar. A 1-oz. jar of parsley flakes costs almost a dollar. Look at the savings!

7. Buying food in quantity saves dollars and cents, but if the extra amount of produce is more than your family can consume before spoilage, dry the surplus. Again, you've saved food as well as money.

8. Make your own convenience foods for really great savings:

Seasoning salts. A blender will powder dried onions, celery tops, garlic, etc., to which a small amount of salt can be added.

Instant soup mix. Powder combined dried vegetables in blender. According to your taste preference, put one or two teaspoonfuls of powdered vegetable mix (carrots, onions, potatoes, celery, turnips, cabbage, tomatoes) in a cup of boiling water and stir. A bouillon cube adds extra flavor.

Salad enhancer. Powdered or flaked dried onion, garlic, cucumber, celery or tomatoes can be sprinkled over salads for extra nutrition and flavor.

Baby food. This can be made from powdered vegetables; two teaspoons per cup of water, then simmered until cooked. Remember that spinach is concentrated, so reduce the amount to about three-fourths teaspoon per cup of water. Tomatoes develop a stronger flavor in drying, so use reduced amounts.

Cornmeal or flour. Dried corn can be ground in a grain grinder to substitute for cornmeal or corn flour.

Parsley flakes. Dry parsley and use in cooked casseroles or soups. Of course, it never becomes crisp again when reconstituted, to be used as a garnish, but the dry flakes can be sprinkled over salad for color and nutritive value.

Dried mushrooms. Keep them on hand for casseroles or soup. Buy when they're on "special" at the market. This adds up to real savings.

Dried grated foods. These are a real time- and money-saver, especially if you have a grater attachment on an electric mixer. It saves fuss and dishwashing too. Store in plastic bags or glass jars for quick availability. Grated foods can be dried in three to four hours in a dehydrator or oven, and then stored. Before using, reconstitute desired amount of vegetables or fruit in boiling water. For example, if the recipe calls for 2 cups of grated carrots, pour 1¼ cups boiling water over about 1¼ cups of dried grated carrots. Let stand 5 to 10 minutes. They will puff up and can be used as required in the recipe. Use any unabsorbed water in the bowl.

Each fall we leave some of our carrot crop in the ground all winter. This keeps them sweet and flavorful. But when spring plowing time comes, they must all come out. These carrots won't keep very long. There's a limit on how many you can give away, and we always wasted quite a few until I discovered that I could scrub (they needn't be peeled), grate, dry, and store them for future convenient use. Reconstituted, they are quickly available for cookies, cakes and salads. For salads, after pouring boiling water over them, place them in the refrigerator to chill and they will become quite crisp.

Grated lemon and orange peel. (See Citrus Fruit, chapter 7.)

Cold remedy. Untreated grapefruit rind can be dried, powdered and stored in a jar for an effective cold medicine. For easy grating, freeze the rind, then it will dry quickly. Put in blender to powder. Put 1 teaspoon of the powder in a cup and pour boiling water over it. Let steep 10 minutes. Pour through a tea strainer into another cup. Add honey and drink.

Dip chips. Cucumbers, zucchini, potatoes, tomatoes and carrots make good dip chips. They can be sprinkled lightly with barbecue sauce or seasoning salt before drying.

Sportsman's energy snack. Instead of candy for a quick-energy pickup, eat dried fruit and fruit leather. Campers, hikers, fishermen, hunters, skiers and hungry school children can stuff a few pieces or a roll of fruit leather in their pockets. Healthful snacks are preferable to greasy potato chips and other nutrition-starved TV fare.

"When dehydrated foods are subjected to normal digestive processes, the blood sugar rises more gradually, maintains a longer peak level, and then gradually declines to signal the need for additional nourishment. In contrast to this, the more concentrated and sweet foods tend to send the blood sugar up much faster, the peak blood sugar time is much shorter, and the letdown is usually much quicker and may be attended by undesirable clinical symptoms.

"The intake, digestion, metabolism and subsequent physiological function of the body is far better with the more natural foods devoid of extra sweets and seasonings. The dehydrated foods offer some very definite advantages and may well take a distinct place in the medical world of good nutrition." [1]

Prepared cereal. Make your own prepared cereals or complete breakfast bars or survival bars. (See chapter 10.)

Drinks. Dried fruits make excellent nourishing drinks. (See chapter 7.)

Herbs. Dry herbs for healthful and refreshing teas. These are costly when purchased in a health food store, but are easily dried at home. Have your own herb garden. Fresh herbs, such as sage, supply fuller flavor in cooking than the powdered product in a can from the market shelf.

Fruit leather. Instead of wasting overripe fruits and vegetables, use them for making fruit or vegetable leather for snacks, or in desserts. Vegetable leathers can be used in soups. (See chapter 6.)

Raisins. Home-dried grapes and cherries make better "raisins" than raisins.

Candies and confections. Dried fruits and fruit leather can be made into a variety of deliciously "different" confections. (See chapters 6 and 7.)

Tomato sauce. Make your own. (See chapter 8.)

Nutritional Value

Much has been published in recent years concerning the people of Hunza in the Himalayas, because they seem to have found the "fountain of youth." Fruit eaten raw in season, or dried for winter use, is a most important part of their diet. Apples, pears, peaches, apricots, black and red cherries and mulberries are grown in large quantities in Hunza.

The apricot is their most valued fruit. They eat not only the flesh but they crack the pit and eat the kernels inside, which furnish much-needed fat for their diet. Since there are few cows and goats to fulfill their daily requirement of fat, the women long ago discovered that the oil from the apricot seed is a rich source of fat. Because apricot oil is such an essential part of their diet, Hunzakut farmers grow more apricot trees than any of the other fruit trees.

---

[1] Jay and Shirley Bills, *Home Food Dehydrating* (Bountiful, Utah: Horizon Publishers, 1974), p. 13.

There is a trace of prussic acid in the seed, an excess of which could be harmful. If a tree produces any trace of bitterness, it is destroyed. Scientists have found this apricot oil rich in polyunsaturated fatty acids.

"Dried apricots are soaked overnight in rich mineral water and eaten with cooked millet or made into a paste as jam for bread; by adding more water, and then mashing, it is made into juice for drinking. The fruit is very sweet, so it serves as a sweetener as well. Apricots have a rich source of organic copper and iron, which might well be the reason for the absence of anemia in the Hunza people.

"Hunzakuts seldom cook their fruit. They eat it raw as it comes from the trees. When we were traveling, our drivers would eat a few apricots, crack the seed open with their teeth, indicating a strong dental structure, eat the kernel and be satisfied. Observing their endurance, there was no doubt in my mind that they were nourished well."[2]

Today our concern in preserving food in any manner is to retain as many of the nutrients as possible, as well as the natural flavor, cooking qualities, and appearance.

Spoilage is due to microorganisms known as bacteria, yeasts and molds. We can and bottle foods at high heat to destroy these microorganisms.

Another cause of food spoilage is enzymes. The enzymes are responsible for ripening fruits and vegetables, and we need enzymes in human nutrition. These enzymes cause changes in color and flavor. If we simply stop their growth instead of destroying them, this is desirable. The drying process accomplishes this, drawing moisture out of the cells, likening the product to a sponge. When the moisture is gone, enzymes cannot continue to function. When moisture is re-introduced to the food, the cells soak up the moisture and enzymes begin to work again. However, do not expect the product to be restored exactly to its fresh form of crispness.

Microorganisms cannot grow without moisture, but they can attack reconstituted food. To be on the safe side, refrigerate reconstituted dried food to retard spoilage. Reconstitute only the amounts you intend to consume in a short period of time. When dried food spoils during storage, you know that sufficient moisture was not drawn out.

What food value is left in dried foods? The chief nutritional losses are vitamins A, C, and D. For the most part, other nutrients remain in the dried food, because they have not been cooked out with high heat. This includes fiber, minerals, and other vitamins.

---

[2] Renee Taylor, *Hunza Health Secrets* (New York: Award Books), pp. 106-107.

6

Why Dry?

At best, vitamin C is an unstable vitamin. It cannot be stored in the body and is not stored in food to a marked degree. It is water soluble and can be lost through exposure to light, air and heat. Do not use soda to preserve color, because the alkali destroys vitamin C. For example, soda added to preserve color in string beans destroys the vitamin C.

Refrigeration helps to preserve vitamin C. For example, orange juice (or a cut orange) left exposed to the air at room temperature loses its vitamin C, although the taste may not be altered. For this reason, keep such foods tightly covered in the refrigerator.

Stored fruits and vegetables (canned or put away in a pit) diminish in vitamin C (ascorbic acid) the longer the food is stored. Canned food stored at 80° F. for one year loses 25 percent of the ascorbic acid. When stored at 65° F. the loss is reduced to 10 percent.[3] Of course, a good part of the vitamin C was already lost in the heat processing. Logical conclusions would be that non-cooked, dried foods, stored in a cool (65° F.), dark place would retain more vitamin C.

Vitamin C or ascorbic acid can be added before drying, as explained in chapter 3, Pretreatment.

Vitamin A is fat soluble and is not lost through cooking water.

Cutting, paring, slicing, etc., diminish vitamins A and C by exposing the flesh to air and light, causing the fruit to darken even before drying. This is called oxidation.

Lest you despair at the losses and feel preservation is a hopeless cause, however, keep in mind that enzymes are continuing to work all the time in the fresh foods purchased in the supermarket. There it sits under strong lights and heat, and the purchaser has no idea how long since it was harvested. For this reason, canned, frozen, or dried foods (processed immediately after harvest) run good nutritional competition with supermarket produce. In addition, you have prevented spoilage of the food, so that it can be stored for a considerable time. Since home-dried foods have not been exposed to high heat or additives, they retain more of the natural nutrition than do cooked foods.

There is considerable controversy over existing food values and bacteria count in dried foods, based on the method and time of drying: sun or oven versus dehydrator, fast dehydrator versus slow, high temperatures versus low, high airflow versus low, preservatives versus natural, airtight storage versus "breathing" containers. In the final analysis, people remain quite convinced that their way is best and are reluctant to change. Consequently, I have simply listed many ways, and it is up to the homemaker to choose what is best in each particular home and locality.

---

[3]Barbara Densley, *ABC's of Home Food Dehydration* (Bountiful, Utah: Horizon Publishers, 1975), p. 23.

Keep your own notebook in which to record details of successes and failures for future reference.

Perhaps of real significance is the fact that food has been dried successfully (that is a relative term) for thousands of years, and human beings have been sustained by it. The Hunzakuts are a good example, since their life span far exceeds ours, and they enjoy good health without ever having heard of sophisticated scientific food testing and methods of preservation.

Controlled heating methods (oven or dehydrator) might give erroneous concepts to homemakers, especially that the food can and should be dried very rapidly. The danger of fast drying is "case hardening." If food is to be dried successfully, moisture must be removed as quickly as possible, but at a temperature which does not seriously affect the texture, color and flavor of the food. If the temperature is too high and the humidity too low, with little airflow, the surface of the food is cooked, and case hardening results, with the moisture trapped inside. Microorganisms can grow in the presence of moisture, so this causes "keeping" problems as well as flavor changes. Low heat and high airflow accomplishes quick drying without case hardening.

Enzyme activity can be retarded or inhibited by heat or chemicals through the use of blanching, steaming, cooking or sulfuring,[4] which are discussed in chapter 3. The faster the growth of the fruit or vegetable, the more active the enzymes present; therefore, the faster they will spoil.

The natural salts and sugars are in a concentrated form in dried foods, and *when reconstituted they require very little, if any, sugar or salt. Never add salt or sugar before cooking,* or toughness will result. Add only enough sweetening or salt to taste.

Form the habit of drinking water when you consume dried food, because it is concentrated, with moisture removed. Dried food is "more-ish." Often more is eaten at one time than is realized. Adequate liquid is a necessary part of digestion and body utilization.

The reason spoilage takes place in preserved foods is that the canning heat is not high enough. Low-acid foods (most vegetables) require higher heat than high-acid foods (most fruits). In canning, pressure cookers should, therefore, be used for vegetables. Hot water bath is sufficient for most fruits.

If spoilage results with dried foods, sufficient moisture has not been removed. Mold and microorganisms can attack it. "Sweet sour" results.

---

[4]Flora H. Bardwell and D. H. Salunkhe, *Home Drying of Fruits and Vegetables,* Utah State University Extension Bulletin, Logan, Utah, pp. 1-2.

Why Dry?

Understanding the Terms

This book is devoted to *home drying* of foods, but the question is frequently asked, "What's the difference between home drying and commercially dehydrated foods?" The terms *drying, dehydrating, freeze-dried* and *low-moisture* are confusing.

Drying or *dried foods* usually refer to home-dried products or those which can be purchased in the supermarket, usually at the produce section. Dried fruit such as that purchased in plastic see-through bags is sulfured to ensure a pliable, chewy fruit, and the moisture content remains at about 20 to 25 percent.

You probably couldn't leave in that much moisture without the food spoiling. Home-dried fruit is usually reduced to about 10 percent moisture content, or even less. Some fruits darken during the drying period. The finished product should be leathery, or even somewhat brittle, minus "moisture pockets" which can be detected with the fingers. Vegetables should be brittle and hard. Don't worry if fruit is dried to the brittle stage, but don't let it scorch. It can be easily rehydrated to the desired stage.

Dehydrating is a commercial process which reduces moisture content (with heat) down to 2 or 3 percent. Commercially dehydrated food has a long shelf life.

Freeze-drying is another way of removing water down to 2 or 3 percent. During the process of freeze-drying, water is removed while the product is frozen, by sublimation. (The ice is changed to vapor without going through the liquid stage.) The food is prepared, then frozen and placed in a vacuum chamber. A small amount of externally applied heat drives out the moisture while the food is still frozen. Refrigeration is not necessary, but freeze-dried food should be stored at cool temperatures and will deteriorate under long storage.

The term *low-moisture* applies to both dehydrated and freeze-dried foods.[5]

Suit Your Own Needs

Many methods and preparations for drying foods are given within the pages of this book. Some are new, others are very old. Experiment and decide what is best for you in your home, with the facilities at your disposal. Weigh the advantages and disadvantages and decide for yourself. As you explore, you will find new adaptations to suit your particular needs.

---

[5]Barbara Salsbury, *Just in Case* (Salt Lake City: Bookcraft, Inc., 1975), pp. 129-130.

Whatever method you choose, the possibilities are vast. Taking advantage of specials will save money. Harvest time differs with various foods, of course.

Grains, seeds, cereals, breads, and confections can all be converted into tantalizing, nutritious snacks, especially with a dehydrator, or even the oven. So develop the year-round habit and reap the benefits. Dry and save!

Chapter 2
METHODS OF DRYING

Listed below are methods of drying food. There are advantages and disadvantages to each method. Experiment and find out what works best for your particular needs and limitations. The important thing to know is that drying can be done by apartment dwellers as well as homeowners who may have lots of outdoor space. Heat and air are the two essentials. Then, of course, you must have something on which to place the food for drying. A simple rack of some kind to suit your own drying facilities is necessary.

Drying Racks

Window screens that will fit your drying space or oven (or even an old screen door) may be used. To construct a rack for drying food, stretch a width of screen, or stainless steel hardware cloth over a wooden frame (any size to fit your drying space) possibly made of ½" × 1" strips. Fit a duplicate wooden frame on top of the screen. (The screen is then sandwiched between the two wooden frames.) Fasten the frames together so the screen is taut and is raised up off the table, even when loaded. It can be easily washed.

If regular screen or hardware cloth is used, cover screen with net and arrange food on the net for easy removal and to prevent snagged fingernails and a metallic taste or discoloration on food, or possible toxicity. Net also helps to absorb the drips from juicy fruit. If drying outdoors, fruit can be covered with another strip of net or cheesecloth to keep it free of insects. If more ventilation is needed under the drying rack, or the screen sags when set on a table, elevate it at the corners with bricks, so fruit doesn't touch the table. Arrange food in one thickness to ensure good air circulation between pieces of food. As food dries, of course it shrinks.

This screen rack is also excellent to place over trays of drying fruit leather on a picnic table to keep off insects. Be sure the screen rack is not so large that it cannot be moved to shelter for the night or during a rainstorm.

Room Drying

If your drying area is large enough, a scrubbed screen door or window screen may be used. Or a drying rack as described above can be constructed small enough to fit your oven. This can be used interchangeably for oven or room drying any time of the year.

Cover the screen with nylon net (preferably white). This catches drips and can be sudsed after each use. Fruit should be turned over about once a day, and fingernails can be ruined if food is stuck to the screen. Cover food with another piece of net or cheesecloth for protection against insects.

Drying racks can be placed:

1. In front of a heating vent.

2. On the warm furnace ducts in winter.

3. On top of the refrigerator.

4. Above the water heater.

5. In a hot car or camper.

6. Outdoors in the sun.

7. In front of a sunny window. A tilt to the sun is best and allows circulation underneath as well. (My kitchen window reaches 115° F. on a cold, sunny day in midwinter, which is ideal for room drying. However, if you have an inquisitive cat, dog or child, this could be disastrous.) A fan helps to circulate air and speed drying. Contamination from the air could be a detriment.

If your kitchen is too humid, another room or the attic would be more desirable. But remember that good airflow is important in whatever area you select.

Fruit slices or rings or string beans may be threaded on heavy string and tied to a line which is strung across a room. Ears of corn can be hung from a line by the husks. When completely dry, it will "rub" off the cob. It's a good idea to winnow it in the wind so the chaff will blow away.

Herbs should not be dried in direct sunlight. Dry them indoors, if preferred, tied in bunches and clipped to a line. Or they can be placed gently in a bag made from net or cheesecloth and hung from a line. Do not overload the bag or they'll not dry, but will spoil and mold instead.

Room drying is not the ideal method, but if weather is bad outside and no dehydrator is available, it can still be done.

Oven Drying

A friend complained that she couldn't dry fruit in her oven—she couldn't imagine why. In response to my questions, she explained that she had placed apple slices on a cookie sheet and barely turned on the oven, but they never dried out—just got mushy. Actually she was slow-baking the apples instead of drying them. *Never* try to dry food with the oven door closed. Moisture must escape. In fact, an electric fan set by the oven door will speed drying, because air is better circulated.

Methods of Drying

Use an oven drying rack as pictured below, since circulation on all sides is desirable. However, if a cookie sheet is all you have, you can still dry food in the oven by placing a piece of plastic wrap over the cookie sheet and then arranging food on it. This prevents reactions from the metal. Observe precautions as listed below.

Four thicknesses of nylon net or some cheesecloth stretched over the regular metal rack in your oven can be used, if not overloaded. The net will not burn if you keep oven heat as low as it should be for drying, 140° F. or below. However, the net may sag between the rungs of the regular oven racks, and this is a nuisance. This ties up the oven for any other use during drying.

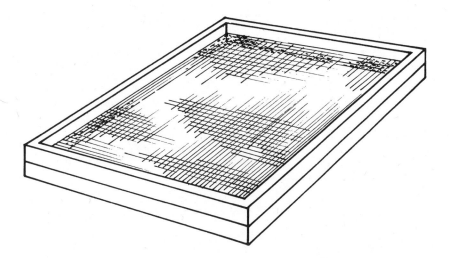

If special oven racks are to be constructed, make sure the outside dimensions are at least 1½″ smaller than the inside width and depth of your oven, to permit good air circulation. Try to use three racks and prop the bottom one on wooden blocks three or four inches high at each corner of the oven floor. Rest one tray on the blocks and two more on the standard metal oven racks. Place them on the upper sliders, allowing at least three inches between each drying rack.

Observe the following precautions for oven drying:

1. Do not overload oven with more than four to six pounds of fresh food at one time. Placing a thickness of net over the screen will save fingernails when turning fruit. This also minimizes messy drips in the oven.

2. Place a thermometer on the top tray toward the back. This is important. Every oven is different, and can change. One night after putting pineapple in the oven to dry, I went to bed feeling confident that

13

the fruit would be just right next morning. *Never* do this! Next morning, even though the oven door was still ajar, the pineapple was burned. After puzzling over the reason, I recalled that the oven element had recently been replaced, and I hadn't realized that it was heating abnormally high. After testing with the oven thermometer, the oven, even with the door open, would not drop below 220° F. I was baking—not drying!

I tested at every level in the oven and finally discovered that I could keep the oven below 140° F. only by turning on the broiler (which should be avoided), using only two trays and keeping them as low in the oven as possible, with the oven door ajar about six inches. Do take the time to test before wasting food.

Prop the oven door open with a folded potholder or a jar ring at the right distance to keep an even temperature. This is essential for air circulation and to permit moisture escape.

3. Keep oven heat below 140° F. Vitamins are destroyed at a higher heat. Dr. Salunkhe of Utah State University states that three times as many vitamins are destroyed at 160° F. as at 140°-145° F.[1]

A gas oven pilot light may be sufficient for drying, as it should be registering 110°-120° F. with the oven door slightly ajar. If you find it necessary to light the flame, turn it as low as possible and check frequently so the flame doesn't go out unnoticed. Keep a gas oven door ajar at least eight inches if flame is lighted. If necessary, use an eight-inch-long stick to prop the door open.

4. Examine the food after three or four hours. Turn food if it's drying and beginning to stick. Turning over the food speeds drying. Rotate trays for even drying.

5. Keep the room well ventilated.

Most vegetables dry in four to twelve hours, depending on humidity, and on the variety and thickness of prepared food. Some fruits dry in the oven in six hours, but it usually takes longer.

Disadvantages of oven drying

1. The oven is not available for other uses. If the oven is needed, just leave the tray of drying food on the table until oven is free again, but this is not a good practice.

2. Only a small amount of food can be dried at one time.

3. If heat is not kept low, the net will ignite. In case of such an accident, quickly close the oven door. Lack of oxygen should smother the flames.

---

[1] Jay and Shirley Bills, *Home Food Dehydrating* (Bountiful, Utah: Horizon Publishers, 1974), p. 17.

Methods of Drying

4. Leaving an oven unattended is dangerous. Be sure you *know* your oven if you leave it on overnight. Over and above the fire hazard, your food may become overdone without being checked periodically.

5. Food dried in the oven is usually more brittle than when dried outside or in a dehydrator, and usually dries a little darker. Fruit leather often becomes "chippy" around the edges, and sometimes the whole sheet becomes brittle.

6. Requires artificial power of some kind, but the cost is usually minimal, as explained in chapter 1.

7. There is no fan in an oven to circulate the air, but all good dehydrators have a fan.

Advantages of oven drying

1. Specially constructed oven racks can be used elsewhere for drying.

2. The oven is available for drying year around.

3. Since only a small amount can be dried at one time, oven drying is ideal for vegetables such as onions, celery tops, parsley, peppers, etc., which would wilt if not preserved in some way. They can be dried for future use instead of wasting. The oven is ideal for grapes or a couple of pineapples which might be on "special."

4. Food is kept free from sudden rainstorms or other water which causes mildew, also free from insects, blowing dirt, or air pollution.

Car or Camper Drying

A car sitting in the sun becomes an oven, as does a camper, even when the weather is quite cool outdoors. Arrange the trays on the seats and back of the station wagon. Blot food to prevent drips and cover the seats and back with an old sheet. Roll windows down slightly to achieve proper heat and permit good air circulation. Fasten net over the openings of the windows to keep insects out. Open the vents of a camper as wide as possible.

Sun Drying

During hot summer days, the sun provides natural heat for drying outdoors.

1. *Clothesline.* Net or cheesecloth can be spread and clipped to the clothesline. Arrange food carefully on the net. This is not very satisfactory,

since the net sags between the lines, like an old mattress, and the food has a tendency to settle and bunch in the middle. Reaching to the height of the clothesline is tiring when food must be arranged and turned. Cover the food with cheesecloth or another piece of net.

2. *Suspended frame.* A wood-framed screen can be suspended with rope or wire from the rafters of the carport or some place which gets sun a good part of the day. Hang it at the right working height for arranging, turning, and removing food. A piece of old white sheet can be spread over the screen. This reflects heat and speeds drying and also soaks up juicy drips.

3. *Old screen doors or windows.* These can be scrubbed and used as makeshift sun dryers and could also be suspended as above. Always cover screen with net.

4. *Screened-in dryer.* Don't expect to construct a sun dryer for nothing, even if scrap lumber and scrap screen are used.

A skillful husband can build a screened-in set of shelves with as many drying trays as desired. These trays should be rotated to different levels to facilitate drying.

Stainless steel hardware cloth is best and will hold up over the years, but is expensive. Ordinary hardware cloth is galvanized. Galvanized screen is zinc- and cadmium-coated and can cause dangerous reactions when it comes in contact with acid fruits.[2]

Fiberglas is teflon-coated, but the woven strands can separate and stick to drying food. Copper screen is not suitable. Aluminum screen may also react to the acid.

Two thicknesses of net spread over any drying surface will keep the food from direct contact with the screen.

Turn the food as it dries, perhaps once a day. This is a good job for children with scrubbed hands.

A drying rack needs a spot to rest. The roof of the carport or garage can be used, if easily accessible. The tilt of a roof toward the sun makes it ideal. The picnic table and benches, or other surface up from the ground, are easy to work with.

Disadvantages of sun drying

1. The sun is not a dependable source of drying energy. Even at best, the sun and outside hot temperatures are not available very many months out of the year in most areas. Of course, air also assists the drying

---

[2] The Food Editors of *Farm Journal, How to Dry Fruits and Vegetables at Home* (Philadelphia: Countryside Press), p. 16.

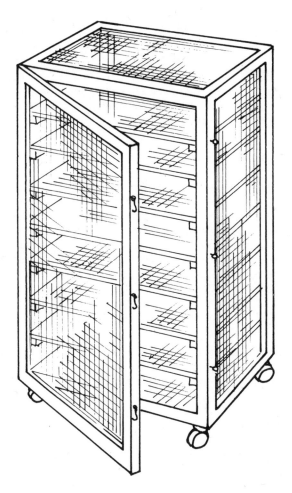

process. Hot, sunny days do not always coincide with food harvesting time, and food continues to ripen whether it suits your convenience or not. There may not be the necessary successive days of good weather, and the prepared food spoils.

2. Space is usually limited by the amount of available drying screens.

3. Summer showers are unpredictable, so drying fruit must not be left unattended. Rain water, sprinkler water, or heavy dew must never reach the fruit. Mildew will result. At night bring the trays into the house, or put under cover of the carport or garage. Never cover drying fruit with sheets of plastic for weather protection. Moisture from the food condenses on plastic and drops down, resulting in mildew.

4. Drying food must be brought indoors during windy and dusty weather.

5. To be sure bacteria has been destroyed, sun-dried food should be pasteurized. Spreading the food on a cookie sheet and heating in a closed 165° F. oven for half an hour will serve the purpose, or it can be placed in the oven in clean bottles covered with new lids, at 165°-170° F. for thirty to sixty minutes (depending on size of jars), so that heat reaches *all* food. Remove bottles from oven and screw lids tight. Pasteurization can also be done by turning up the temperature of the dehydrator and setting the bottles inside for the same time.

Solar Drying

A solar dryer can be made by placing an old window (a plastic pane is better than glass) above the food which is drying on the rack. This intensifies the sun's rays and raises the temperature. However, do not permit condensation on the glass. Moisture drops back on the food, causing mildew. Allow several inches of space between the glass and the food so that the air can circulate. A fan nearby aids circulation, but could be a nuisance outdoors. Do not let the heat rise above 140° F. under the glass. Some solar dryers are manufactured with one glass side to capture the sun's rays. Usually a fan is installed inside the cabinet to move the warm air out. Be sure the heat chamber is properly vented for moisture escape.

White fabric (old sheeting) placed over the screen intensifies the sun's rays and becomes a form of solar heating. Extremely juicy fruit sticks to the fabric, and cotton fibers sometimes stay on it.

Dehydrator

Habitually I referred to my dehydrator as my "dryer." Then one day a friend said, "I never dreamed you could dry fruit in a clothes dryer." My mouth dropped open. Can't you visualize all that fresh, juicy fruit being tumbled around in a clothes dryer? We must be specific. Technically, only large commercial equipment should be called a dehydrator. However, to avoid confusion in the average homemaker's mind, let's call an electric home dryer a dehydrator.

A dehydrator is not a necessity, but is a real advantage if you intend to do much in the drying field. A dehydrator consists of a heating chamber, a heating element and a fan. The element maintains heat and the fan circulates the air inside the chamber and forces the warm moist air out through vents. A dehydrator protects the food from insects and pollution. With low heat and fan, the moisture is removed and forced out through vents. This is the basic principle of good dehydrators. However, engineering makes some of them more efficient than others. Ask yourself if the investment will add up to real savings in the amount of available food for preservation.

18

Methods of Drying

Do investigate thoroughly before deciding on the one which will best serve your needs. Both portable and large dehydrators are available.

The do-it-yourselfer can't stand to pay the price of a manufactured dehydrator. Some individuals are extremely skilled and knowledgeable, but too often the "home expert" spends a great deal of time deliberating over prospective plans. Next the right materials must be sought through extensive shopping, at an expenditure of much more time. Parts must usually be mail-ordered and there may be a long waiting period. By the time the dehydrator is finished, the harvest season has come and gone. Nor are materials for a homemade dehydrator cheap. Some ingenious men have converted old refrigerators or freezers into effective dehydrators. But when you add up the time and money, you may discover it would have been an economy to purchase a tested manufactured dehydrator. All too often, the homemade variety ends up with faulty engineering (especially with poor airflow and shelves too close to the heating element), and the food is either burned or not dried quickly enough. Frankly this is a job for the experts.

In purchasing a dehydrator, consider the following points:

1. *Inside drying capacity.* Remember that advertising pictures are deceiving. First consider inside drying space and drying capacity. One small dehydrator is available which advertises that it has 2300 cubic inches of inside space. This sounds like a lot, but it will dry only one-sixth of a bushel at a time and the airflow is very poor.

This means a homemaker must prepare a small amount of food many times. A certain amount of clutter and muss in the kitchen always results with each preparation. Even if the food were to dry in twenty-four hours, which is seldom the case, the remainder of the bushel must wait—for days. During the waiting time, the food will deteriorate in quality and eventually will spoil. Also, each one-sixth of a bushel means the same fuss and cleanup on each day—even if the food didn't spoil while waiting. It's much simpler to take care of the whole bushel at once and clean up the kitchen only once.

2. *Economy.* A low purchase price of a dehydrator doesn't always mean high economy. Produce purchased by the case or bushel is always less expensive than by the pound. Therein lies economy. However, if part of the food spoils because of lack of drying space, that's waste. Also a homemaker's time should be worth something. Any dehydrator costs money. So weigh purchase price of available dehydrators and compare advantages and disadvantages of each. The needs of each home differ, as do homemakers' time schedules, according to workload and size of family.

The cost of operating a good dehydrator is usually minimal, and shouldn't require any more power than a television set to operate.

3. *Construction.* Is it sturdy? Were reliable, high-quality parts used? Can elements and thermostats be replaced? How easy is loading and unloading? Does the unit lose all its heat through the loading cycle? Can it be kept clean? Are vents open "doors" for insects? Are such vents screened? What material is used? Wood will warp, splinter and sliver under moisture and heat and, of course, is combustible. Is the heating element covered for safety? Metal construction diffuses heat into the room. Insulation will conserve energy and keep the surrounding area comfortable.

4. *Shelving.* Are the edges dangerously sharp? Do they slide in and out without upsetting the load? What material is used? Metal shelves (except for stainless steel) cause chemical reactions, discoloration and sometimes bad taste. Screen shelves sag with the load and must be handled very carefully. Perforated plastic shelves are durable. Be sure they are food safe. (Refer to "Screened-in dryer.")

5. *Uniform controlled temperature.* The temperature should be as constant as possible to ensure continuous drying. I prefer lower (110°-120° F.) heat for some foods, especially for herbs and leafy greens.

Avoid "case hardening."

The unit should be pre-heated to the top heat allowed by the thermostat. When the dehydrator is loaded with cool, juicy fruit, of course the inside temperature drops markedly. As the moisture is drawn out by the fan and heat, the inside temperature slowly rises until the fruit is dry, and the temperature will again reach the maximum heat allowed by the thermostat. You may want to reduce the thermostat temperature setting for the latter part of the drying. Fruit usually takes much longer to dry than most vegetables because of sugar content.

6. *Airflow.* Proper venting and airflow through the chamber permits warm, moist air to be expelled.

Humidity affects the drying, as does the warmth of outside air. Never expect drying to be speedy if humid, cool air is being sucked in. For example, a unit placed on the patio by the lawn will draw in humid air from the grass, and the drying process virtually stops at night; then one wonders why the food spoiled.

When night temperatures reach about 60° F., outside drying is almost stopped during night-time.

Always operate a dehydrator in a well-ventilated area. Spare bedrooms, attics, basements, heated garages and kitchens can all be used year-round if the cabinet does not emit too much heat for comfort. Also, pungent odors (onions especially) may be a problem indoors.

7. *Carefree operation.* Does the dehydrator require babysitting? Many units demand that the shelves be rotated constantly because of the

20

Methods of Drying

difference in heat in the top and bottom. Food on the top shelf can spoil while the food on the bottom shelf will be overdone, if not rotated.

If you were looking for a new automobile or sewing machine, you'd shop around and compare the different makes. Follow the same procedure with a dehydrator. Don't let a salesman "sell" you. Compare points and be your own boss.

21

Chapter 3
PRETREATMENT—PRESERVATIVES, ANTI-DARKENERS AND DIPS

The word *preservative* is distasteful to many people. I have successfully dried most fruits in the sun, oven or dehydrator, retaining excellent color without the use of anti-darkeners or preservatives. Bananas especially need an anti-darkener if the color repulses you or your children. Preservatives can help in retaining color and vitamins, especially in sun drying. However, they are unnecessary when using a dehydrator. Longer drying time causes food to darken, due to oxidation. Since sun drying takes longer, the food is usually darker than when dried in a dehydrator. Also, some dehydrators take longer than others.

It is impossible to recommend universal treatment and procedures, because of differences in humidity, climate, home setups, and variables in the food itself. Listed below are a number of suggestions. You must experiment to see what works best specifically for you.

Ascorbic Acid

Ascorbic acid can be obtained from the druggist for the purpose of retarding oxidation and preventing darkening of light-colored fruits during drying time. Dissolve 1 tablespoon of ascorbic acid in 1 gallon of water and dip fruit in this solution for 2 minutes only. Drain or place food on paper towels to absorb excess moisture.

Fruit Fresh is one well-known brand name for ascorbic acid and is much more expensive than purchasing from the druggist or another supplier that you might discover in your own locality.

Sulfuring

There is much objection to sulfuring by natural foods enthusiasts, but if you wish to prepare your fruit this way, here are two methods known as "sulfuring indoors."

Sodium bisulfite solution

(Do not confuse with sodium bisulfate, which may cause diarrhea.)

Sodium bisulfite helps to prevent darkening during storage. Not all druggists carry it. Use 1 tablespoon of sodium bisulfite to 1 gallon of water. Dip fruit for only 2 minutes in solution and drain. With paper towel absorb as much moisture as possible and set fruit out to dry.

Combination of sodium bisulfite and ascorbic acid

Use 1 tablespoon of sodium bisulfite and 1 tablespoon of ascorbic acid in 1 gallon of water to dip fruit for 2 minutes only. This helps to preserve quality and color during dehydrating process as well as during storage.

Outdoor sulfuring

Bardwell and Salunkhe of Utah State University suggest the following procedure for sulfuring fruit outdoors:

1. Place fruit on wooden trays having wooden slats, with the fruit not over one layer deep on each tray. Place the fruit with the skin side down to prevent loss of juices. (Metal will react with the sulfur, so it is imperative that wooden trays be used.)

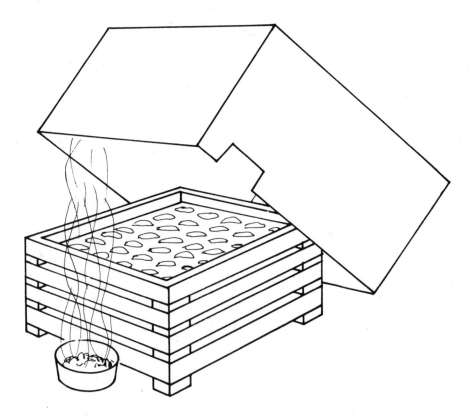

2. Stack the trays about 1½ inches apart to permit the sulfur fumes to circulate.

3. Use a tight wooden box or heavy cardboard carton to cover the trays. For circulation purposes, it should be slightly larger than the stacked trays.

4. Cut a small opening at the bottom of the box for lighting the sulfur and for ventilation.

5. Place sulfur in a clean metal container such as a tin can [tuna can is ideal], shallow but deep enough to prevent overflow. To each pound of prepared fruit, use 2 teaspoons of sulfur if sulfuring time is less than three hours; 3 teaspoons of sulfur if the sulfuring time is three hours or longer.

6. Set the can beside the stacked trays and set fire to the sulfur. Do not leave the match in the can. It may keep the sulfur from burning up completely. Avoid the fumes, which are irritating.

Sufficient space should be allowed for the sulfur to burn freely. This should be no less than three inches of space between the metal can holding the sulfur and the stacks of wooden trays, and between the can and the inside of the carton or covering.[1]

Sliced apples should be sulfured ½ hour.

Apricots should be sulfured 1 hour.

Peaches and nectarines should be sulfured 1 to 1½ hours.

Pears should be sulfured 2 to 2½ hours.

Sulfuring will ensure a soft, pliable product, if that's what you prefer. The taste is objectionable to some people. Sulfured fruit should be rinsed before reconstituting. Never use the trays from your dehydrator in the sulfuring box. Never use your dehydrator for sulfuring. Be sure to set dehydrator in the open air outside when drying sulfured food. Sulfured foods should never be dried indoors, as the fumes are irritating.

Salt Solution

Soak fruit for 10 minutes in a solution of 4 to 6 tablespoons salt to 1 gallon water. Drain in wire basket or colander. Rinse thoroughly and drain again. Place clean turkish towel or several thicknesses of paper towel on the counter and blot dry. Set out to dry on racks or screens. This works for oven drying also. The salt solution is the least desirable treatment, but salt is readily available in any kitchen. Rinse dried food before reconstituting for use.

---

[1] Flora H. Bardwell and D. H. Salunkhe, *Home Drying of Fruits and Vegetables*, Utah State University Extension pamphlet, Logan, Utah, pp. 4-5.

Honey and Lemon Juice

Squeeze a lemon and combine the juice with 2 tablespoons honey. Bottled commercial lemon juice works just as well. Honey may have to be heated slightly to make it very runny. Put mixture in a tightly-covered bowl and fill halfway with prepared apricots (or other fruit). Tumble ever so gently until fruit is well coated. Take to the drying rack and "pop the backs" (turn the pitted half almost inside out between your forefingers and thumb) of apricots or plums as you arrange them. Two or three thicknesses of net, placed directly over the screen or rack and under the fruit, helps to hold the drips. The net can be sudsed out for re-use. But you must know this is a sticky process.

Pineapple Juice

Dip fruit in canned pineapple juice to retain color. This also gives the fruit a distinctive flavor.

Pectin Solution

Mix 1 quart water, 2 quarts sugar, 1 package pectin, and juice of 2 lemons. Stir well to dissolve. Coat fruit thoroughly. Drain well in colander. Put out to dry. Cover with net or cheesecloth. Don't throw away the remaining liquid after dipping. Combine with equal amount of sugar, boil and use for pancake syrup.

Syrup Solution

Dixon Ford of Farmington, Utah, has been quoted almost every year in the Salt Lake City newspapers for his method of dipping apricots. With his permission, I am quoting his recipe, although it differs slightly from the newspaper accounts.

Combine 1½ cups sugar, ½ cup light corn syrup, 1½ tsp. ascorbic acid powder (Fruit Fresh works fine) with 2 cups water. This amount will coat half a bushel of apricots. Heat the syrup ingredients just long enough to dissolve the sugar, then cool.

Spray apricots clean with water and allow to dry thoroughly. Cut apricots in half and dip immediately in cool syrup. Set a colander in a bowl and drain apricots. Re-use the liquid that has dripped into the bowl.

Arrange on drying rack, cut side up so halves barely touch. Cover with net or cheesecloth. Allow to dry 2½ to 3 days in direct sunlight. [If you pop the backs they'll dry in half the time.] Turn. When apricots are dry around edges and quite leathery, place in a brown paper sack one-fourth full. Fold top down and hang sack from the clothesline for a day or two. Agitate at least once a day. This equalizes the apricots so that those that have dried too much absorb moisture from the others as their moisture pockets disappear. When fruit is rubbery like raisins, pack in quart jars. They have retained a good orange color. Mr. Ford has stored apricots like this in a cool, dark storage spot for four years and they have darkened only slightly. He reports that they are not hard, and that they are more tasty than candy.

Half a bushel of apricots makes about 2½ to 3 quarts of dried apricots.

Note: Pop the backs of apricots to speed drying. "Popping their backs" means to gently turn the apricot- or plum-half almost inside out, breaking up the tight fibers around the pit which hold the moisture.

Steaming or Blanching

Blanching means to precook the food either in boiling water or in steam.

The *steam method* preserves more food value than "boiling water blanching." Place the food in a steam basket (refer to Equipment in chapter 5), with boiling water underneath but not touching the food. This pre-cooking should be done just long enough to stop enzymatic action, and set to cool. Refer to charts for time for each vegetable. Do not pack the basket with food, but allow the steam to circulate freely around the food. (This is also the best way to cook fresh vegetables.)

If a Tutti-Frutti (see Equipment) is not available, pour water into a deep pan large enough to accommodate your steaming basket. Place no more than two inches of water in the bottom and bring to a boil. Set the basket in the pan, but be sure the boiling water does not touch the vegetables. Cover tightly and let steam the required seconds or minutes. Vegetables are blanched when heated through and limp or wilted. But do not overblanch, especially greens, or they will mat and not dry well. To test for doneness, cut through the vegetable. It should look translucent nearly to the center. It should feel soft but not cooked. Spread steamed vegetables on paper towels to cool.

For *boiling water blanching,* fill the kettle with enough boiling water to cover vegetables. Small amounts should be used so the water doesn't stop boiling. Boil vegetables the shortest time possible to heat them through. Use the same water for successive batches of food, adding more water as necessary, but keep it boiling. Drop vegetables in and retrieve with a sieve or slotted spoon. Test for doneness the same as for steam blanching. Chill immediately in cold or ice water. Drain on paper towels.

27

Many vegetables must be steamed or blanched to stop enzyme action. Although some nutrients are lost in both processes, steaming is recommended over water blanching. The difference is that the food is treated with steam from the boiling water, but the water does not touch the food.

A Tutti-Frutti is an excellent steaming appliance. (Refer to Equipment.)

Gilding the Lily

If you have a dehydrator, there are many ways of giving a variety of flavors to dried fruit. Dried fruit is already concentrated natural sugar, but if you want to impress your family or friends with a special sweet treat, below are a few ideas. Let your imagination take off and you'll come up with some new combinations:

1. Cinnamon and apples go together like bread and peanut butter. Sprinkle apple rings lightly with cinnamon.

2. Different flavors of gelatin powder straight from the package can be sprinkled on lightly. Combine flavors with fruits as you desire, i.e., raspberry or strawberry gelatin for apples and pears, lime or lemon for pears or peaches, orange for plums, etc.

3. Sprinkle bananas with shredded coconut or nuts (but do not store, because rancidity develops from coconut and nuts). Powder coconut in blender and sprinkle lightly on apple slices. Toast coconut in oven on a cookie sheet until lightly brown and powder in blender for still a different variation.

A fertile mind can dream up all sorts of concoctions. Dream on!

Chapter 4
STORING DRIED FOODS

Equalizing Moisture

A frequent question is, "How can you tell when it's dry enough?"

After fruit has dried for the specified length of time, some parts, especially the edges, are brittle and hard, while moisture pockets can still be felt with the fingers. Of course, the food needs "equalization."

Remove the fruit from the drying rack. Place no more than a quart or two into a large paper sack, being sure the quantity does not pack down. Fold over the top of the bag and pin to the clothesline. Every time you step into the back yard, give the sack a quick pop on the bottom to redistribute the fruit inside. After two or three days on the line, the moisture will be equalized, and the fruit can be stored.

Never, never put warm fruit directly in storage containers. Always let the food cool completely before packing.

Pasteurization

If fruit has been dried outside in the sun, you should pasteurize it, especially if it was subject to air pollution or insects. Spread fruit on a cookie sheet and bake fifteen minutes at 165°-175° F. Remember that more vitamins are destroyed at this temperature than at the drying temperature, which should not exceed 140° F.

Food can be pasteurized in glass jars also. Place the dried food in absolutely clean glass jars that are completely dry. Fill to the top. Screw on the lids loosely. Place jars on oven rack so jars won't touch and break, in a preheated oven 165°-175° F. Leave in oven thirty to sixty minutes, depending on size of jars, so that heat penetrates to the center. Remove from oven and screw lids down tightly, which creates a partial vacuum. Don't worry if the lid doesn't pop down to indicate a seal. Fruit will remain quite soft and pliable during storage.

Use this method for storing all dried foods, shelled and unsalted or untreated nuts, raisins and coconut. This preserves freshness and avoids rancidity.

Leather (see chapter 6) can be stored in jars and sterilized as explained above, but roll it *without* plastic wrap or waxed paper. Cut the rolls the necessary length to fit the jar size used. Wide-mouthed peanut butter jars are excellent. Use the same lid.

Some of my friends have had their fruit and vegetables go wormy or weevily. This is probably because sufficient moisture was not extracted. In a dehydrator there is probably no contamination problem. However, if food was dried in the sun, there is the possibility that flying insects could have laid eggs on the food. This is the reason for pasteurization, to kill any enemy to successful drying. Eggs hatch in warmth and moisture. It is therefore better to remove too much moisture rather than too little. Food can be easily rehydrated to the desired consistency. Airtight containers also help. Any container which permits air circulation could contribute to this danger.

Storage Guidelines

Proper storage is most important. Recommending specific guidelines is difficult because of variable humidity and temperature factors in different localities. Humid climates present a storage problem. Also insect infestation is more prevalent in some areas than others. Both of these factors are enemies to successful storage. In dry climates, storage isn't difficult if cleanliness is observed.

Cool, dark, dry are the key words for successfully storing anything in order to prevent deterioration. This is true of canned as well as dried foods.

Never place storage containers of any kind directly on a cement floor. If shelves cannot be constructed, run long two-by-four-inch strips of wood on the floor, so that cans or other containers have air space under them. Do not place storage containers flush against a cement wall. Leave a little air space.

Dried fruits and vegetables will deteriorate in color, flavor, texture and odor and for best results should not be stored longer than a year. For experimental purposes, I have stored fruit much longer with minimum visible deterioration. Learn to label and rotate.

Be sure storage containers are absolutely clean and free of any odors. Do not store by other odoriferous products, such as gasoline or oil.

Check dried food occasionally, especially leather, to see if it is molding. If you find mold, the food may not have been sufficiently dried, or moisture is somehow getting into the storage area. Remove pieces with mold. Heat the rest of food in the container in the oven for thirty minutes at 165°-175° F. Use this food as soon as possible.

Fill storage containers completely to crowd out the air inside.

Storing Dried Foods

Kinds of storage containers

1. Clean metal cans (such as shortening cans) with tight-fitting lids. These keep out light, moisture, air and insects.

2. Clean plastic containers with tight-fitting lids. These do not keep out light. Sometimes mice nibble through plastic, so it is not foolproof.

3. Plastic bags. Heavy heat-sealable bags keep out moisture and air, but not light, and should be stored in boxes or at least in heavy brown paper sacks for darkness. Check your hardware store for convenient heat-sealing units, which are also ideal for freezing. "Self-sealing" or "locking" heavy plastic bags are available in the supermarket, but these are not as heavy as heat sealing bags.

Store the right amount for one meal for your family in each bag, so that only small amounts are used at a time and the container is not half full of air. Insert a straw in a small unclosed space of the lock bag and suck out excess air. Use two plastic bags if small sandwich "baggies" are all you can obtain. Then place the sealed or tied bags in a paper sack for darkness. Be sure to label and date clearly. Some fruits look quite similar when dried. This is especially true of fruit leathers.

Never use plastic bread wrappers. A friend was shocked to see that all her apricot leather molded after three weeks of storage. Her SOS was too late then. When I probed the possible reasons, she explained she had stored it in plastic bread wrappers. The molds from bread were already present and were just waiting to attack the fruit leather or dried fruit. Too bad!

Do watch for insect infestation. Eggs can be laid on plastic bags and, when hatched, they eat right through. Only you know your conditions.

4. Glass jars. Even if you don't wish to pasteurize your dried food, glass jars are excellent storage containers. Put a paper sack over them for darkness.

5. Sacks, cloth or paper. If you are not bothered with insects or vermin, fruit leather can be rolled in a sheet of plastic wrap, or waxed paper, then placed in paper sacks or cloth bags. Remember that long storage deteriorates color, flavor and quality, especially if no more protection than this is given. But it's good to know that in an emergency or severe shortages, you can store in this simple manner.

6. Freezer. Dried fruit and leather can be stored in the freezer. Wrap and seal well in plastic wrap so moisture cannot get inside. Remove only the amount needed. I never store fruit leather in the refrigerator. It goes hard and chippy for me, but others store successfully that way.

If fruit leather turns chippy, don't throw it out—fruit chips are tasty too. To soften fruit leather almost to its original consistency, rinse out a plastic container with tight-fitting lid. Drops of water will adhere to the walls of the container. Put the leather in. Fit the lid in place, and leather will soften in a day or two. A new plastic bag may also be used in the same way.

If dried fruit is too brittle to please you, place fruit in a sieve and run water over it. Allow water to drain and place fruit in a glass or plastic container. Cap tightly and set in the refrigerator overnight. Fruit will then be soft and chewy. *Do not* store this fruit again, but consume it.

Vegetables

Vegetables should be stored in much the same manner as fruits, though vegetables are more vulnerable to insect infestation than fruits. Be sure to keep them *dark, cool* and *dry*.

Chapter 5
BEFORE YOU START TO DRY FOOD

Equipment

Some items are listed by brand name and the source, to save mutual correspondence and telephone time.

Colander or food mill
Stainless steel paring knife (to keep food from turning dark)
Grater (The grater attachment on an electric mixer is a lifesaver.)
Food chopper (It has two blades criss-crossed.)
Vegetable slicer (adjusts to different widths)
Apple sectioner
Apple corer
Drying rack (Can be used for oven drying and also for room drying and sun drying. If you are to eventually build a dehydrator, make oven racks that will fit into the one to be constructed.)
Screen (See chapter 2, Methods of Drying)
Net, preferably nylon
Steaming basket (stainless steel fan-type is good)
Mehu-Liisa, more commonly known as a Tutti-Frutti juicer-steamer (European made). Ideal not only for juicing but for steam-blanching food before drying. This is available in a few hardware stores. Bob and Greta Ashdown, 612 E. Pheasant Way, Bountiful, Utah 84010, have the franchise in the United States. Contact them for details.
Kitchen timer
Blender
Cookie sheets (or TV trays), about 17″ × 12″, for drying leather.
Plastic wrap
Masking tape, for labeling storage containers
Cherry stoner (The plastic one made in Germany is best. It pops out stone without crushing cherries. Contact Stak-On International #10 South 100 East, Sandy, Utah 84070.)
Kitchen scale
Food grinder
Measuring cups
Oven thermometer
Storage containers

Equivalents

General (English Conversions)

a pinch or dash = less
   than 1/8 tsp
3 tsp = 1 tbsp
2 tbsp = 1/8 cup
4 tbsp = ¼ cup
5 tbsp plus 1 tsp = ⅓ cup
8 tbsp = ½ cup
12 tbsp = ¾ cup
16 tbsp = 1 cup
1 liquid oz. = 2 tbsp
½ pint = 1 cup
1 pint = 2 cups
2 pints = 1 quart
4 cups = 1 quart
4 quarts = 1 gallon
8 quarts = 1 peck
4 pecks = 1 bushel
16 oz. = 1 lb.
16 liquid oz. = 2 cups
28 grams = 1 oz.
454 grams = 1 lb.
4 cups flour = 1 lb.
1 cup all-purpose flour = 7/8 cup
   stoneground whole wheat flour
2 cups granulated sugar = 1 lb.
2¾ cups brown sugar = 1 lb.
1 cup granulated sugar = 1 cup
   brown sugar or 1 cup raw sugar
1 cup molasses = 13 oz.
5 large eggs = 1 cup
8 egg whites = 1 cup
16 egg yolks = 1 cup

2 cups butter = 1 lb.
4 cups grated cheese = 1 lb.
1 cup uncooked rice = 2
   cups cooked
1 cup uncooked macaroni = 2
   cups cooked
1 cup uncooked macaroni = 1¼
   cups cooked
1 large lemon = ¼ cup juice
1 medium orange = ½ cup juice
2 cups dates = 1 lb.
3 cups dried apricots = 1 lb.
2½ cups prunes = 1 lb.
2½ cups raisins = 1 lb.
1½ lb. apples = 1 quart
3 large bananas = 1 lb.
1 cup nut meats = 5 oz.
1 lb. potatoes = 4 medium-
   sized potatoes
1 lb. tomatoes = 3 medium-
   sized tomatoes
1 egg is equal in leavening
   power to ½ tsp baking powder
1 lb. dried vegetables = 8-12
   lb. fresh vegetables
1 lb. dried fruit = 4-8 lb. fresh
1-2 cups dried food reconstituted
   will serve about 6 portions

Kitchen Math with Metric Tables

Measure	Equivalent	Metric (ml. = milliliter)
1 tbsp	3 tsp	14.8 ml.
2 tbsp	1 oz.	29.6 ml.
¼ cup	4 tbsp	59.2 ml.
⅓ cup	5 tbsp plus 1 tsp	78.9 ml.
½ cup	8 tbsp	118.4 ml.
1 cup	16 tbsp	236.8 ml.
1 pint	2 cups	473.6 ml.
1 quart	4 cups	947.2 ml.
1 liter	4 cups, plus 3⅓ tbsp	1,000.0 ml.
1 oz. (dry)	2 tbsp	28.35 grams
1 lb.	16 oz.	453.59 grams
2.21 lb.	35.3 oz.	1.00 kilogram

Chapter 6
FRUIT AND VEGETABLE LEATHER

Fruit leather (sometimes called jerky) is a revival of an old preservation method.

Encyclopedias provide little enlightenment on its origin, nor can I find any old book which treats that subject. A 1933 edition of *Compton's Encyclopedia,* (Vol. A, p. 233, under *Apricot)* shows a picture of three Syrian men standing beside "stacks of apricot leather" which, it says, will be used to make jams and sauces. I haven't yet experimented sufficiently to develop such recipes, but am sure it can be done.

The botanical name for "apricot" is "prunus armeniaca." Going on the assumption that the apricot, and hence apricot leather, must have an Armenian root, I wrote to my good friend George Mardikian, the distinguished chef-owner of Omar Khayyam's of San Francisco fame. My inquiry brought an enthusiastic response:

"Apricots are so plentiful in Armenia and they were a lifesaver for the Armenians. We claim that our country was the place where the Garden of Eden was located, and that it was an apricot which Eve gave to Adam, not an apple. I can still recollect coming down from the high mountains into the valley of Ararat and getting this beautiful aroma of the apricot. It was just like entering a garden of beautiful flowers.

"The Armenians used apricots for many purposes. They dried the pulp on sheets of cardboard. [No doubt it was oiled to keep the juices from penetrating the cardboard. An oiled surface would allow it to be peeled off.] Our parents would cut up a big piece and roll it and give it to us for in-between dinners as a sustainer. Armenians cooked a great many of their pilaffs with apricots. Then we also made stews of them, as well as sauces and jams.

"This is an ancient way of preserving fresh fruits in all forms, from apricots to mulberries; but apricots, I suppose, are the best of all."

Another friend, who cannot verify her source, explained that fruit leather was made when people had to crush it in hollowed-out rocks, the same way they ground grain, and then spread it out in the sun to dry on skins. When dry, it could be peeled off easily and stored for the winter.

If no blender or electricity is available, fruit can be forced through a food mill, colander, ricer, or sieve. A food mill is much easier to use than a colander. However, using raw fruit requires generous amounts of "elbow grease." If the fruit is cooked, it is much easier to handle in this way. But thank goodness for blenders which can puree raw fruit almost instantly with no "elbow grease" at all.

Since fruit ripens quickly, and drying requires prime-condition produce, the question always arises of what to do with overripe fruit and the bits and pieces not fit for bottles or dryer. Leather is the happy answer. The riper the fruit (within reason, of course—not spoiled) the sweeter the leather. Since the product must be reduced to puree anyhow, flavor is the important consideration. If the fruit is too bland, add additional flavoring, sweetening and/or spices, or a combination of fruits, etc.

If extra sweetening is needed, always use honey if possible. Avoid the use of white sugar because the resultant leather will tend to be granular and will usually go hard and chippy. Corn syrup is a good substitute for honey. Brown sugar gives a pleasant taste variation and doesn't tend to result in "chippiness" as much as white sugar.

Instructions in most leather recipes requires cooking all fruit first. Cooking produces a smoother product but decreases nutrients and increases the time, work and muss of preparation as well as the chance of scorching the fruit. Also the leather tastes cooked. I prefer not cooking, not only because of convenience, but because more nutrients are preserved. Why increase your workload? There are, however, exceptions. Some fruit requires cooking to reduce fiber and to retain good color.

For oven drying of leather, be sure to check Oven Drying in chapter 2 for testing your oven, and other precautions. Oven drying requires surveillance. Keep the oven door open as in drying fruit. Do not go to bed at night thinking the leather will be perfect next morning. It will probably be overdone. This is seldom a problem in the dehydrator, unless the thermostat is set very high.

When you can loosen the edges with your finger and then pull the leather completely free of the plastic wrap, it's done and resembles a piece of pliable leather, hence its name.

See chapter 4 for proper storing. However, that's the problem— seldom is there enough to store, because of big and little nibblers. Do check the stored leather occasionally for mold—also to see if it's still there! If it's beginning to mold, it wasn't sufficiently dry. After a year or two of experience, you'll know what's the best method for your particular home and locality. Humidity does make a difference, but can probably be overcome with a little patience and persistence.

Never use waxed paper on which to pour puree for drying. The moisture congeals the paper to the fruit and who wants to eat paper? Foil (oiled sparingly) can be used on the cookie sheet, especially with oven drying, but plastic wrap is best. For easier removal, always ease leather from plastic wrap or foil while still warm. Otherwise it may stick.

Fruit and Vegetable Leather

you still have too much puree, put it in freezer containers and freeze until space and time are available. Or, if necessary, process in hot bath as you would to bottle fruit, but you needn't add sugar. Of course, the resulting leather has a slightly cooked taste, but this is not objectionable. In this way you can make fresh leather all winter, drying in a sunny window or in front of heat vents. A fan speeds drying.

Though they are not necessary, you may add flavorings as desired for variation, such as:

Vanilla extract
Almond extract
Lemon extract

Spices: cinnamon, nutmeg, cloves,
pumpkin pie spice
Tang
Unflavored gelatin

When making juice or juice for jelly from plums, cherries or grapes, after simmering the fruit and draining off the juice, puree the skins and pulp and make leather. Sweeten as necessary with honey. If you are lucky enough to have a Tutti-Frutti (see chapter 5, Equipment), the pulp left in the steaming pan can be pushed through the holes or put through a colander, and it's ready to dry and is probably already sweet enough. If pits were removed before steaming, simply put the pulp in the blender and proceed as usual for leather. Use ¼ cup pineapple (fresh or canned) for better color and flavor. Leather is as versatile as fruit varieties.

Apple

Sweeten as necessary. Early apples (Transparent, June, Astrachan) are especially good, but scarce. Any apples can be used, even if they must be cooked slightly first. If apples are not juicy enough to puree well, or are too firm, add 1 or 2 tablespoons of lemon juice or pineapple juice. This enhances flavor and ensures a light color. Apples usually remain quite chunky and may not have sufficient moisture to be pureed.

You may prefer cooking the apples slightly to soften them, with just enough water to prevent scorching.

Variations:

Add ¼ teaspoon cinnamon or nutmeg or vanilla. Mix with other fruit. Add ½ cup coconut to 2 cups puree. Delicious! Add a few chopped nuts.

Coconut and nuts go rancid, so do not store, but you won't have a chance to. You'll wonder where it disappeared to.

Combine apples or applesauce with orange juice or tangerine juice.

Applesauce

No sweetening is necessary. Canned "old" applesauce liquefied in blender makes delicious leather. Use same variations as listed under "Apples."

Apricot

Sweeten only if apricots are too tart. Do not peel.

Variations:

Chopped walnuts.

Cinnamon or nutmeg.

Brown sugar instead of honey.

Puree ½ cup crushed or fresh pineapple, and use as part of the total 2 cups per cookie sheet.

Banana

No sweetening. Puree bananas, 2 cups per cookie sheet. Chopped nuts may be added for variety.

Blueberries, blackberries and mulberries

Because of their blandness, combine with other fruits and flavorings, as desired.

Cherry

Sweetening is optional, depending upon ripeness and variety. Pit. (See Equipment for cherry stoner.)

Two tablespoons lemon juice helps to retain color. However, cooking or steaming preserves the color better. Cook in small amount of water to prevent scorching, then proceed according to basic instructions.

Warning! Cherry leather often retains moisture and takes several days to dry. It also sticks badly to plastic wrap. If you have trouble, lightly-oiled foil might serve you better.

Variations:

Add 1 teaspoon almond flavoring to 2 cups puree. Cherries may be combined with raspberries, black raspberries, apples, pineapple or rhubarb.

Use 1 cup cherry puree and 1 cup puree of other fruit. Put berries through a strainer if seeds are objectionable.

Royal Ann cherries can also be used. They produce a fairly light-colored leather of fine texture.

Fruit and Vegetable Leather

Cranberry-date

Dates provide the necessary sweetening. Soak 1 cup pitted, chopped dates in enough water to cover. Soaking time varies with the softness of dates. Blend this combination until quite smooth. Gradually add 1 cup cranberries and blend until smooth. Dry as usual.

Grape

1. Combine equal parts of apples and seedless grapes. Add honey to taste.

2. If you've bottled Concord grapes whole in the bottle and have old ones on hand, drain in a colander set in a bowl. Let juice drain off. Push through the colander or food mill, and you have puree for leather. (See General Instructions.)

Grapefruit

Wash and peel grapefruit. Remove as much white membrane as possible because this adds bitterness, but don't try to get rid of it all. Separate the sections. Remove seeds. Puree. Add honey—start with 1 teaspoon and add to suit your taste. Use only 1½ cups puree and don't let it get near the edges of plastic wrap, or it will seep underneath to discolor the cookie sheet. Then it smells terrible.

Lemon

Scrub and peel lemons. Separate sections. Remove seeds. Puree 1¼ to 1½ cups. Add honey, as needed, starting with 1 teaspoon per cup of puree. You may need 2 tablespoons honey, according to your sweet or tart tooth. If it's too runny, add 1 tablespoon gelatin to give it body. Set out to dry. Observe same caution about the edges as with grapefruit.

Note: Save scrubbed lemon peel, which hasn't been sprayed or treated, and freeze. Then grate and dry for any recipe calling for grated lemon peel. It should always be reconstituted in an equal amount of hot water to heighten flavor.

Limon

Combine limes and lemons and proceed as for lemon.

Nectarine

Follow recipe for peach.

Dry and Save

Peach

After scalding, draining, and removing skins and pits, puree 2½ to 3 cups per cookie sheet. Usually needs no sweetening.

Peach-pineapple

Liquefy ½ cup pineapple and 1½ cups peaches per cookie sheet. No sweetening necessary.

Pear

Skins may remain, but this makes leather a bit grainy. Core. Put 1 tablespoon water in blender, then add pears a half at a time. Puree 2 to 2½ cups per cookie sheet. No sweetening. Pineapple enhances flavor. Use ½ cup pineapple for part of puree.

Pineapple

Liquefy crushed or fresh pineapple and use 2 cups per cookie sheet. No sweetening.

Pineapple-strawberry-rhubarb

Sweeten to taste. Puree ¾ cup each of crushed pineapple, strawberries, and rhubarb. Simmer strawberries and rhubarb together until tender in just enough water to keep from scorching. Puree all three together in blender.

Plum

Plums vary greatly in taste, sweetness, and color. Some varieties are clingstone, others freestone. Italian prunes are in the same family. Start with 1 teaspoon honey and add more as needed to suit your taste.

Extra juicy plums need 1 tablespoon gelatin added to puree to thicken.

Use 2 cups per cookie sheet.

Plum leather sometimes takes a long time to dry and remains tacky and very hard to remove from the plastic. You may find it necessary to use a sheet of lightly-oiled foil rather than plastic. Be sure to remove while still warm. After pulling it off initially, turn it over and dry longer. If leather is still very sticky, roll without plastic. For serving, cut with scissors in "rounds."

44

Fruit and Vegetable Leather

Plum-apricot

Place one sheet of plum leather between two sheets of apricot leather and roll together. Superb!

Raspberry

Sweeten with honey or corn syrup to taste.

May be used plain or combined with bananas, apple, pineapple, or wild huckleberries.

Seeds are a problem to some people and you may wish to simmer first and put through a strainer.

Rhubarb

Begin with 1 tablespoon of honey to sweeten.

Cut in small pieces. Puree 1½ cups raw rhubarb. Use only ½ cup rhubarb to begin the liquefying process. Add a tablespoon of water if necessary. Juice does not blend with the fibers. Pour onto plastic wrap on cookie sheet. Spread with tines of a fork, and be sure juice does not spread to the edge.

Raw rhubarb produces a strange kind of leather which may "turn you off." It looks very unappetizing and tastes woody at first but it grows on you—perhaps.

A totally different product results from simmering cut-up rhubarb in just enough water to keep from scorching. When rhubarb is tender, puree it and sweeten to taste.

Rhubarb can be combined with black raspberries, cherries or strawberries. Frozen strawberries are excellent and can be used as they come out of the container, already sweetened.

Persimmon

Puree and sweeten to taste, a little less than 2 cups per cookie sheet. Combine with other fruits as desired.

Uses of Fruit Leather

Snacks.

Confections. With scissors snip "rounds" of leather (not rolled in plastic wrap). Dip these rounds in carobcote for nutritious "chocolates." (Carobcote is a coating substitute available in most health food stores.) For variety, press an almond, pecan or walnut half in the middle of the "round" and dip in carobcote.

Leather can be reconstituted (pour ½ cup boiling water over ¾ cup cut-up leather and let stand 5 minutes). Whirl in blender. It can then be added to ice cream, malts, yogurt, puddings, and pies. For example, reconstituted apricot leather can be added to a package of vanilla Whip 'N Chill for a delicious pudding or apricot pie filling. Or it can be added to your favorite apricot chiffon pie recipe.

Fruitlets

You've enjoyed aplets and cotlets? Make your own variations.

PEARLETS

½ cup cold pear puree	½ cup honey
2 tbsp gelatin, dissolved in puree	1 tsp vanilla
¾ cup pear puree	nuts (optional)

Dissolve gelatin in ½ cup puree. Boil on medium heat ¾ cup puree and honey for 10 minutes, stirring occasionally to prevent scorching. Combine both mixtures and cook 15 minutes longer, stirring constantly. Remove from heat. Add coarsely chopped walnuts and 1 tsp vanilla. Pour into lightly buttered loaf pan and let stand overnight in refrigerator. Loosen edges with knife. With pancake turner, lift under edges until it will come free. Place on cutting board. Cut in long strips and store, cutting into pieces just before serving. Store in refrigerator. You may roll squares in cornstarch or powdered sugar.

Variations of this same recipe:

Aplets—use applesauce	Strawblets—use strawberry puree
Cotlets—use apricot puree	

PLUM PEARLETS

Make recipe as for Pearlets. Cut into long strips. Roll the strips as tightly as possible in plum leather. If desired, with your hands, work cornstarch into the outside to keep it from being so sticky when wrapped. Roll in waxed paper. Slice off serving pieces as needed. If this confection is to be stored for quite a long time, leave out the nuts.

This is a real company treat!

LEATHER PINWHEELS

Spread contrasting colored filling over a sheet of leather. Roll like a cinnamon roll and slice. For example, spread Light-Colored Filling over plum or grape leather. Or Dark-Colored Filling over apple, Royal Ann cherry, or pear leather.

Light-Colored Filling:

½ cup liquid honey
1 cup non-instant dry milk
1 tbsp butter
½ tsp vanilla

½ to 1 cup coconut
½ cup chopped nuts (optional—
   peanuts, cashews, sesame
   seeds)
½ cup ground apples or
   pears (optional)

Stir, then knead honey, dry milk, butter and vanilla together. Add remaining ingredients and spread on sheet of dark fruit leather. Roll, Chill before slicing. If there is any left after serving, store in the freezer.

Dark-Colored Filling:

½ cup ground dates
1 cup ground dried cherries
1 cup chopped walnuts
1 tbsp lemon juice

1½ tbsp honey
1 tsp finely grated reconstituted
   orange rind or lemon rind
   (optional), *or*
   1 tsp lemon extract flavoring

Mix together thoroughly and spread on light-colored leather. Roll. Chill before slicing. If there is any left after serving, store in the freezer.

Tomato Leather

Wash and cut tomatoes. Cook with only enough water to keep from sticking. Put through a food mill or colander, discarding seeds and skins. Boil the paste down until it is fairly thick. Spread this sauce on plastic wrap and dry as other leather. This can be scored and cut into smaller pieces, then rolled into balls. Drop the ball into soup.

Or, for tomato sauce, reconstitute by pouring just enough boiling water to cover the pieces of leather in a bowl. Let stand 5 minutes. Whirl in blender if necessary to make a smooth sauce and use in your favorite recipes requiring tomato sauce.

A Note About Sugar

Sugar in recipes frequently presents problems. Some recipes simply are not successful made with honey. On today's market, raw or brown sugar is simply white sugar with molasses added. This obviously changes the flavor and texture and adds back the nutrients from the molasses. So when "sugar" is specified in one of the recipes in this book, you may prefer using a "natural sugar," such as "turbinado," instead of white sugar to insure a light-colored and flavored product.

A Note About Flour

Stoneground whole wheat flour is usually specified herein, not because it contains more nutrients, but because the product is usually finer and fluffier than burr or roller whole wheat flour, therefore the results are more satisfactory.

Chapter 7
DRYING FRUIT

Dried fruit is a natural sweet-tooth satisfier. The moisture is extracted from the fresh product, leaving only the solids, including sugar, but in a concentrated state. This is why dried fruit tastes so sweet. Mentally if you reconstructed the fruit to its original size, you'd discover that you're also consuming condensed calories. For example, a six-inch round of fruit leather is the equivalent of a large peach. So, although you'll know you're consuming nutritious food, if you have a weight problem, you can't eat as much dried fruit as you may wish.

And do drink water with it.

Have you checked the price of dried fruits in the supermarket? You can enjoy them at a fraction of the commercial cost.

But since home-drying is a new-old procedure, there is a lot of confusion in homemakers' minds. A friend called one day, disturbed because her new dehydrator was full of Italian prunes. They had been there for two days and nights and weren't even beginning to shrivel yet. We slit them open, removed the pits, then quartered them, and they dried without spoiling. That was risky.

So, let's consider some rules for drying fruit. (See also preparation charts at the end of this chapter.)

1. *Open the fruit to the air* through paring, cutting, or breaking the skin by steaming or blanching. Most vegetables and a very few fruits must be steamed or dipped before drying, to preserve color and nutrition. But most of the food value remains—much more than when the food is cooked and sugar is added. (See chapter 3, Pretreatment.)

Wash, remove pits, and "pop the backs" of fruit such as apricots and plums. "Pop" means to halve the fruit and place it pit side to the forefingers. With the thumb, gently turn the fruit-half inside out through your fingers. This breaks up the tight fibers around the pit which retain the moisture. They will dry in half the time and consequently will retain better color and flavor. If apricots are very large, they should also be quartered.

Skins of apricots, peaches, nectarines, and pears are objectionable to some people. If you feel it necessary, remove them. Sometimes scalding peaches will turn them dark. Of course, leaving on the skins whenever possible preserves nutrients. Apples which have been heavily sprayed or waxed should be peeled.

2. Cut fruits and vegetables to a uniform thickness of about ¼". This saves time and handling, because they all dry at about the same time. (See chapter 5, Equipment.)

3. Store properly. See chapter 4 on Storing. Rotate stored fruits and vegetables. If we ever experience severe shortages, it's satisfying to know that we will be able to eat well on dried foods and storage products. And, after all, that satisfied appetite does contribute to our emotional and physical well-being.

4. Bruised or overripe fruit may turn black. Make it into leather.

Use of Dried Fruits

Most dried fruits can be ground and combined to make mouth-watering confections. (See recipes in this chapter.)

Snip with the scissors and add to cooked cereal a few moments before serving.

Snip and sprinkle over granola.

Use in gelatin for salads or desserts. Reconstitute by covering dried fruit with boiling water. Let stand five minutes. Drain. Fold into partially set gelatin.

Grind and use for fillings for cookies and cakes.

Dried apples make excellent snacks. Reconstitute and simmer for desserts, or whirl in the blender for applesauce.

Dried apricots make nutritious snacks and can be soaked and used in drinks, as well as recipes. (See Recipes.)

One year most of my "drying" friends had their apricots discolor. Some of them had black portions, but the flavor was not affected too much. This was the only year I know of this happening. Only part of mine went black. But use those black ones ground up for a new variety of raisin in cookies. Your children will never know.

Dried avocado can be reconstituted and used as bits in salads. Chill in refrigerator after reconstitution for a crisper consistency.

Dried bananas are yummy snacks. When dried brittle, they can be crushed to powder in the blender or hammer mill. This can be used as flavorings for desserts, salads, etc. Dried banana slices or strips can be reconstituted and used in recipes calling for fresh bananas.

Dried berries can be ground into powder for flavoring and coloring for desserts and salads. Make fruit syrups out of berry powder. Reconstitute the powder in boiling water and let stand five minutes. Then add more water as desired. Combine this "juice" with an equal amount of sugar and boil about ten minutes, or until it begins to thicken.

Dried cranberries can be reconstituted and put through a sieve for a delicious drink. They can be chopped before drying and then reconstituted and used as fresh cranberries in salads calling for cranberries.

Drying Fruit

Dried cantaloupe and other melons are best simply as snacks.

Dried cherries make better raisins than raisins. The cherry stoner listed under Equipment is fast and fun. So I leave my cherries whole. If I had to pit them singly, or had to sun dry them, I'd cut them in half for quicker drying. Cherries are good snacks or can be used in recipes. (See Recipes.) Before putting them through the food grinder for use in cookies and cakes, let them stand a few minutes in hot water so they won't clog the food grinder. Leave them whole for fruit cake or for your favorite bread recipe.

Pie cherries are excellent for pies and cobblers.

Royal Ann or light cherries give color and flavor variation.

Dried citrus fruits. A perfect stranger called me long distance from Arizona to ask what she could do—her freezer was full of lemon juice and still she had more fruit and hated to waste it. So I experimented. Citrus fruits look awful when dried. Reconstituted citrus fruits leave much to be desired. However, pureed in the blender they are better than I had hoped. Lemon leather is a happier solution to the problem than drying the lemon sections.

Dried dates are well known as a delicacy for snacking or to use in recipes.

Date sugar can be made by removing pits, cutting up the dates, drying to the brittle stage, then powdering in the blender. If dates are not sufficiently dried they will clog blender blades and burn the motor. Use for a natural sweetener on cereals, ice cream, etc.

Dried fruit mix can be made at home instead of buying the high-priced commercial "Tutti-Frutti." (Don't confuse this with the Tutti-Frutti juicer described in Equipment.)

Dried grapes can be used for raisins or in salads. Seedless green grapes, after being steamed or blanched, dry to a beautiful gold-green color and are a good substitute for expensive "golden raisins."

Dried guava can be used as snacks or reconstituted, then chilled for use in salads.

Dried papaya can be used as snacks or reconstituted, then chilled for use in salads.

Dried nectarines can be used the same as peaches.

Dried peaches can be used for snacks or reconstituted and used in recipes. (See Recipes.)

Dried pears make delicious snacks and confections or cookie fillings. (See Recipes.)

Dried persimmons can be used for snacks or in any recipe calling for persimmon flavors.

51

Dried pineapple is the best snack in the world! Reconstitute and chill it for use in fruit salad, or mix with other fruit puree or drinks to lighten the color. Do not use in gelatin preparations. Like fresh pineapple, it prevents "setting up."

Dried prunes or plums are excellent snacks or can be used in recipes. (See Recipes.)

Dried rhubarb can be reconstituted and used in many delicious recipes to give the illusion of a "breath of spring" during those cold winter months. (See Recipes.)

Dried watermelon is strictly snack food. It does not reconstitute to the original crisp product you're accustomed to but is, nevertheless, a tasty treat.

Recipes

Note: When substituting honey for sugar in your favorite recipes, observe some adjustments.

Use honey in place of sugar to keep cookies and cakes moist and fresh. When using honey to replace sugar, reduce in half the liquid in the recipe.

When honey is substituted in baked goods, add ½ teaspoon baking soda for every cup of honey used and bake at a lower temperature.

BASIC STEWED FRUIT MIX
(Great fare for campers)

3 cups dried fruit: prunes, apricots, apples and/or raisins,
cherries

3 cups boiling water
2 tbsp sugar (optional)

Snip or chop fruit, if desired, to speed cooking. Pour boiling water over dried fruit and let stand 5 minutes. Simmer a few minutes until tender and plump. Add sugar after cooking. Makes 4 to 6 servings. Can be eaten "as is." It's delicious spooned over granola.

Variations:

½ tsp cinnamon *or*
  ½ tsp pumpkin pie spice

2 tbsp blanched almonds
½ tsp grated lemon peel

FLAVOR-ADDED RICE

Rice may be cooked in a flavorful liquid such as equal parts of tomato juice and water, or even fruit juice to acquire an entirely different appearance and taste.

For a tasty combination, use raisins or nuts or olives added to your rice dishes.

For dessert: Cook with apple juice (half water and half apple juice to complete necessary liquid for cooking). Simmer, stirring occasionally to prevent sticking or scorching. Add dried apples and/or apricots during part of cooking time. Reconstitute fruit with a small amount of boiling water before adding to cooking rice.

Cook with pineapple juice (half water and half pineapple juice to complete necessary liquid for cooking). Simmer, stirring occasionally to prevent sticking or scorching. Add dried pineapple bits during part of cooking time. Reconstitute pineapple with a small amount of boiling water before adding to cooking rice.

For a nutritious main dish: Simmer rice with tomato soup. Cook rice with half the required amount of water first, then add tomato soup to complete cooking. Stir occasionally to keep from scorching. Sprinkle in a few dried tomato flakes or slices. Dried grated carrots and dried chopped onions and peppers, reconstituted in boiling water for 5 minutes, can be added. Add chopped peanuts.

FRUIT OATMEAL

Cook oatmeal as usual. Use old-fashioned or quick-cooking oats as preferred, but old-fashioned are never as "mushy" and have more flavor. However, they require longer cooking.

Just before serving (but long enough for fruit to heat through) fold in one or more cut-up dried fruits: dates, banana chips, raisins, cherries, pineapple, apples, prunes, apricots, pears, grapes. For extra protein and chewing, chopped nuts may also be added. Serve with whole milk for a "stick-to-the-ribs" breakfast.

Depending upon the basic grain of your favorite cooked cereal, it can be fortified by combining a small amount of cornmeal, cracked wheat, oatmeal, or millet.

FRUIT COBBLER (Basic mix)

2 cups dried fruit*	2 tsp baking powder
2 cups boiling water	½ tsp salt
1½ cups sifted flour	3 tbsp butter or margarine
2 tbsp brown sugar	1 egg, well beaten, plus milk to make 1 cup liquid

Pour boiling water over fruit and let stand 5 minutes. Sift together dry ingredients twice. Blend in butter with pastry blender. Add liquid and blend, but don't beat. Spread batter over prepared fruit and bake at 350°-375° F. until fruit is tender. Serve with whipped cream, if desired.

*Use apples, plums, peaches, cherries, pie cherries, or apricots.

53

DRIED-FRUIT FILLED COOKIES

(Here's a filled cookie that doesn't have to be rolled out—it's only half the work.)

Filling:

1 cup chopped dried pears with skins	1 tsp cinnamon, *or*
½ cup brown sugar	½ tsp nutmeg
2 tbsp flour	½ cup chopped nuts
½ cup water	

Combine brown sugar, fruit, flour and water in saucepan and cook over medium heat until thickened, stirring constantly. Add spice and nuts after cooking.

Cookie Dough:

1 cup soft butter or margarine	½ tsp soda
1 cup brown sugar	½ tsp salt
2 eggs	1 tsp vanilla
3 cups sifted all-purpose flour (stoneground whole wheat preferred)	1 tsp cinnamon, optional
	½ tsp nutmeg, optional

Sift together flour, soda, salt and spices. Cream butter, sugar and eggs. Add vanilla. Beat. Add sifted dry ingredients and mix together well. With hands, mold into a long smooth roll about 2½" in diameter. Wrap in waxed paper and chill until stiff (several hours or overnight). With sharp, thin knife cut in thin slices about ⅛" thick, or thinner if possible.

On a greased cookie sheet place the rounds with sufficient space so they won't touch when baked. Put a teaspoon of filling on each round. Then put another dough round on top. Bake 12-15 minutes at 350°-375° F. Makes about 2½ dozen cookies.

CAPPED FRUIT-FILLED COOKIES

Filling:

2 cups ground or chopped dried fruit*	¾ cup water
½ cup sugar	½ cup chopped nuts

Cook together slowly, stirring constantly, until thickened. Cool.

*Dates, pears, apples or apricots may be used. A tablespoon of flour may have to be added to anything but dates. A teaspoon of pumpkin pie spice may be added to pears or apples for a delicious taste variation.

Cookie dough:

1 cup soft butter or margarine
1¾ cups brown sugar
2 eggs
½ cup water

1 tsp vanilla
3½ cups sifted whole wheat flour
½ tsp salt
1 tsp soda
Dash cinnamon

Sift together flour, salt, soda and cinnamon. Cream butter, brown sugar, and eggs. Beat. Stir in water and vanilla. Add sifted dry ingredients and blend well. Drop with a teaspoon onto an ungreased cookie sheet, making a slight indentation in the middle. Place about half a teaspoon of filling on dough. Cover with a cap of another half a teaspoon of dough. Bake at 350°-375° F. for 10-12 minutes. Makes about 5 dozen cookies.

These freeze well, but they also remain in excellent condition for several days unfrozen.

FRUIT-FILLED BARS

Filling:

3 cups chopped or ground dried
  fruit*

¼ cup brown sugar
1½ cups water

Cook over low heat, stirring constantly, until thickened. For fruits other than dates or ground cherries or raisins, a tablespoon of flour may have to be added for thickening. Cool.

*Use dates, cherries, pears, apples, apricots or prunes.

Crust:

1¾ cups sifted all-purpose
  flour (whole wheat preferred)
½ tsp soda
1 tsp salt

¾ cup butter or margarine
1 cup brown sugar
1½ cups quick-cooking oatmeal

Sift together flour, soda and salt. Mix butter and sugar together and add sifted dry ingredients. Stir in oatmeal. Mix thoroughly. Place one-half of this crumb mixture in greased, floured 9″ × 13″ × 2″ pan. Press and flatten with hands. Over this crust spread cooled filling. Cover with remaining crumb mixture, evening it out with hands. Bake 25-30 minutes at 375°-400° F. or until lightly browned. While warm, cut into bars and remove from pan. Makes about 2½ dozen 1½″ × 2″ bars.

DRIED FRUIT TARTS

2 cups dried fruit*
1½ cups boiling water

¼ cup sugar or honey
Pastry for 2 9″ pie shells

Pour boiling water over dried fruit and let stand 5 minutes. Simmer until tender. Add sweetening. Drain off any unabsorbed juice. Roll pastry in oblong and cut into 3″ to 4″ squares. Spoon filling in center of squares; moisten edges and bring corners up on top, pressing together. Bake at 375°-400° F. for 20-30 minutes or until golden brown. Makes 8 tarts.

*Use apples, peaches, apricots, prunes, cherries, pie cherries, or plums.

FRUIT BREAKFAST DRINK

½ cup dried apricots*

2 cups apple juice

Soak apricots in apple juice overnight in refrigerator, then put through blender until liquefied.

*Try other dried fruits of your choice. Experiment!

FRUIT MUFFINS

⅓ cup dried blueberries*
⅓ cup boiling water
2 cups sifted whole wheat flour
⅓ cup honey
3 tsp baking powder

½ tsp salt
1 cup milk
1 egg, beaten
⅓ cup oil

Pour boiling water over dried fruit and let stand 5 minutes. Sift together twice the flour, baking powder and salt. Beat egg. Add milk, oil and honey and blend in dry ingredients. Drain fruit and fold into batter. Spoon into well-greased muffin tins. Bake 20-25 minutes at 375°-400° F. Makes 12.

*Raisins, dates, currants, ground cherries or cranberries can be used.

DRIED FRUIT CRISP

2 cups boiling water
4 cups dried apple slices*

Topping:
½ cup sifted flour (whole wheat preferred)
¼ cup quick-cooking oatmeal

¼ cup butter
½ tsp cinnamon
¼ cup brown sugar (optional, not necessary)

Pour boiling water over apple slices and let stand 5 minutes. Mix together remaining ingredients. Put apples, including unabsorbed water in greased deep pyrex pie plate. Sprinkle topping over apples. Bake 40-55 minutes at 325°-350° F. Serve warm or cool, plain or topped with whipped cream or a dab of vanilla ice cream. Serves 6.

Drying Fruit

Dried apples are concentrated, therefore are sweet, making the addition of sugar unnecessary, unless you have a very sweet tooth.

*Substitute other dried fruits: rhubarb (soaked and simmered first for 10-15 minutes) or plums. A little additional water may be required, because you want juice covering bottom of baking dish.

GERMAN FRUIT BREAD (HUTZELBROT)

Hutzel is the German word for wrinkled fruit (dried fruit). Here's another way to use a combination of dried fruits, also a way to salvage that old dried fruit that may be dark and brittle. After baking, wrap tightly and refrigerate for at least two days for flavors to mellow. Or freeze. It will keep for a month or two. Toasted for breakfast, it's especially delicious. You may want to slice the loaf before freezing and remove only the slices needed for a meal, so it will last longer.

2 tbsp (2 pkgs) dry yeast
4 cups assorted dried fruits
  (apples, apricots, peaches,
  pears, prunes, cherries)
1 cup apple juice
1½ cups warm water
  (about 110° F.)
½ cup honey
2 eggs, beaten
2 tsp salt
1 tsp ground cloves

½ tsp ground cardamom
1 tsp fennel seeds, whirled in
  blender
1 tsp anise flavoring
½ cup wheat germ
½ cup oil
About 7 cups sifted flour
1 cup dates, coarsely cut
1 cup nuts, coarsely chopped
  (walnuts or unblanched
  almonds)

Snip dried fruit coarsely. If fruit is very dry, first pour 1½ cups boiling water over it and let stand 3 or 4 minutes. Drain. Then snip with scissors. Don't throw away the water. Drink it! Put yeast in warm water to dissolve and add honey. Heat apple juice and pour over snipped fruit. Set aside. Juice will be completely absorbed. To yeast mixture add beaten eggs, salt, spices, flavoring, wheat germ and oil. Stir together and mix in 3½ cups of flour. Beat at medium speed for 5 minutes. Gradually mix in 2½ cups additional flour with wooden spoon (or an electric mixer with dough hook). Turn out dough onto a floured breadboard and knead until no longer sticky, adding flour as needed. Place in a greased bowl, turn over. Cover and let rise in a warm place until doubled, about 1½ hours.

Stir dates and nuts into the fruit mixture. Turn dough out on a lightly floured board and knead gently. Flatten or roll to a circle about ½" thick. Spread about half the fruit mixture over dough and knead gently, pulling dough over top of fruit as you gradually work it through dough. Add flour, as needed, to keep from sticking badly. Try to keep a soft dough for better bread. Again flatten dough and knead in remaining fruit as before.

(Recipe continued next page)

Shape into two large loaves. Cover lightly and let rise in a warm place until doubled, about 1 hour. Lightly brush loaves with melted butter. Bake at 300°-325° F. until bread starts to pull away from sides, about 1 hour. Place a piece of foil over the loaves to keep top from burning and the pieces of fruit from becoming brittle. Remove foil the last 15-20 minutes so bread will brown nicely. Turn out loaves on rack to cool thoroughly before wrapping.

STEWED DRIED-APPLE COMBO

1 cup dried apple slices or rings
4 cups boiling water

1 cup dried fruit of your choice*

Pour boiling water over fruit. Let stand 5 minutes. Simmer until tender. Add water as desired to make juice. Add sweetening only if necessary. Serve hot or chilled.

*Combine apples with raisins, dried cherries, dried prunes, dried apricots.

GOLDEN FRUIT CUP

1 cup dried apricots
1 cup dried pineapple*
2 cups boiling water
½ cup (scant) sugar
3 tbsp minute tapioca
Pinch of salt

1 cup (or small can) apricot nectar or apricot juice
3 cups light-colored fruit juice: peach, pear, apple, or more apricot juice
1 ripe banana, sliced

Wash dried apricots, cut in small pieces. Pour boiling water over dried apricots and pineapple and let stand 5 minutes. Cook in same water until tender. Add sugar. Drain liquid into a saucepan and set fruit aside. Bring liquid to a boil and sprinkle in tapioca. Cook until clear. (Cornstarch may be used to thicken the juice slightly if tapioca is not available.) Add additional juices and cooked fruit. May be served hot or cold. If cold, chill thoroughly. Just before serving, add sliced banana.

This may be served as an appetizer, a main dish, or a dessert. If serving as a main dish or dessert, pour a little thin cream over the concoction, or dabs of whipped cream or yogurt may be added. Serves 10-12.

Other light dried fruits may be added as desired: apples, peaches, pears.

* 1 cup or small can of crushed pineapple may be used instead of dried pineapple, and reduce water by 1 cup.

FRUIT CAKE

Here's a recipe for using bottled fruit which has been on your storage shelf for two or three years and is somewhat discolored. Don't waste it. Use it.

1 cup brown sugar or 7/8 cup
  honey*
2 cups sifted whole wheat flour
1 tsp salt
1 tsp soda
2 tsp baking powder
2 tsp cinnamon
½ tsp cloves

½ tsp ginger
2 cups drained "old" fruit, pureed
½ tsp nutmeg
2 eggs
¾ cup oil
1 cup each of raisins, dried
  cherries, *or* grapes
1 cup nuts

Sift together sugar, flour, salt, soda, baking powder, and spices. Beat eggs and oil until creamy. Add drained pureed fruit and dry ingredients. Beat until smooth. Add raisins and cherries (or grapes) and nuts. Bake in 2 greased and floured loaf pans 30 minutes at 350°-375° F. Note: If using honey instead of brown sugar, add it to fruit after it has been pureed. This cake is rich enough without frosting.

*If using honey, and puree measures 1¾ cups, add ½ cup more of flour.

FAVORITE FRUIT CAKE

2 cups currants
1 lb. dates, pitted and cut
2 cups dried cherries
2 cups dried figs, optional
2 cups dried apricots, snipped
2 cups dried prunes
2 to 3 cups nuts
Grated rind and juice of
  1 orange and 1 lemon
6½ cups sifted whole wheat flour

1 tsp baking powder
1 tsp cloves
2 tsp cinnamon
2 tsp salt
3 cups brown sugar
1½ cups butter
6 eggs
½ cup molasses
½ cup sour milk
1 tsp soda

Combine in very large container the currants, dates, cherries, figs, apricots, prunes, and nuts. (If apricots and prunes are very dry, reconstitute with a little boiling water for 3 to 4 minutes.) Mix juice and grated rinds thoroughly and pour over mixed fruits. Sift together twice the flour, baking powder, salt and spices. Cream butter, sugar and eggs. Dissolve soda in sour milk and add with sifted dry ingredients and molasses. Combine batter and fruits thoroughly. Divide batter into 4 loaf pans (9¼" × 4¾" × 2¾" inside top measure), well greased and floured. Bake about 2 hours at 300°-325° F. or until toothpick inserted in loaf comes out clean.

(Recipe continued next page)

Place a pan of water on the bottom rack of the oven and the cakes on the rack above. Place a sheet of foil over the cakes. These two precautions permit thorough baking without drying out and the fruit morsels from becoming brittle on top. Wrap well in plastic and store or freeze.

SURVIVAL OR BREAKFAST BAR

¾ cup honey
½ cup dry milk, non-instant
¼ cup whey powder
½ cup protein powder
½ cup sesame seeds
½ cup wheat germ

½ cup quick-cooking oatmeal
½ cup peanut butter, optional
¼ cup chia seeds
2 cups dried ground fruit
    (choice of combinations of
    apricots, apples, prunes,
    cherries, plums)

Boil honey to the hard ball stage, 250° F. on a candy thermometer. Combine dry milk, whey, wheat germ, oatmeal, sesame seeds, sunflower seeds, and chia seeds. Add honey to dry ingredients. Mix. Add dried fruit and mix well with hands. Mold into bars. Bake 10-12 minutes at 275°-300° F. Do not overbake. These can be dipped in carobcote if desired.

PICK-ME-UP PATTIES

¼ cup peanut butter
¼ cup honey
½ cup whey powder
½ cup wheat germ

½ cup quick-cooking oatmeal
½ cup sesame seeds
½ cup broken cashews or peanuts

Combine all ingredients. With hands, form into dollar-size patties. Place on plastic wrap on dehydrator shelf. Dry until quite firm. Remove plastic wrap and dry until it holds shape well and doesn't crumble. *Or* bake at 250° F. until firm. Do not overbake.

Dipped in melted carobcote, this is a yummy candy.

GRANOLA CANDY

3 cups granola
1 cup instant protein powder
½ cup sunflower seeds
½ cup sesame seeds

½ cup coconut
1 to 2 cups chopped nuts (walnuts,
    pecans, etc.)
½ cup peanut butter
1 to 1½ lbs. carobcote, melted

Grind granola. Add protein powder. Grind coconut, sunflower and sesame seeds together. Add to first mixture together with nuts. Put this mixture into melted carobcote to which peanut butter has been added. Stir well and pat into greased dripper pan to set up. Cut and serve.

CAROBCOTE

Carobcote is a substitute for dipping chocolate and is made from carob powder, oils and brown sugar. It can be purchased at health food stores.

To melt carobcote: Using a doubleboiler, get the water boiling hot, then set it off the burner and put the top of the doubleboiler containing the cut-up carobcote over the water. Put the lid on the doubleboiler and let it set 10 minutes or until it is melted. *Never* let boiling water be under the carobcote—it will granulate and turn streaked as it cools. A marble slab for dipping candy is ideal. Otherwise simply dip nuts, etc., in the pan in which you have melted the carobcote.

DRIED FRUIT CANDIES

1. Put dried fruit in hot water and drain immediately so it will slip through the food grinder easier. Grind and place in separate bowls a wide variety of dried fruit: dates, figs, raisins, cherries, prunes, peaches, grapes, pears, apricots, apples. Combine varieties for different flavors, such as dates, raisins, cherries and pears. Then in another bowl combine apricots, prunes and figs. Add coconut and/or chopped nuts (peanuts, almonds, cashews, walnuts, pecans).

Reconstituted grated or ground lemon or orange rind adds a delightful flavor. Roll these different combinations into balls. Balls can be eaten plain or rolled in turbinado sugar, date sugar, or toasted powdered coconut, or dipped into melted carobcote.

For variety, mold some of the dried fruit around a whole nut and dip in carobcote.

2. Combine several kinds of ground dried fruit, coconut and nuts and stir melted carobcote into the mixture. Form the mixture into long rolls which can be coated with coconut or graham cracker-granola crumbs. Chill and cut in slices.

3. Peanut butter can be added to the carobcote before forming into rolls.

4. Clusters. Drop ground dried fruit and nuts into the carobcote and spoon clusters onto waxed paper.

61

GORP

Mix together dried fruit (whole or cut), seeds (sesame, pumpkin, sunflower), salted nuts, coconut flakes. Use any combination available and the amounts you personally prefer. Keep in a covered container in the refrigerator and put small amounts in candy bowls as serving requires.

Yummy snack food!

FRUIT CANDY

1 cup pitted dates
1 cup dried apricots

1 cup dried seedless green grapes
1 cup sunflower seeds

Rinse apricots and grapes in water so they'll go through the food grinder easier. Put all ingredients through the food grinder. Mix thoroughly and put through a second time. Pinch and roll into balls. Roll in grated coconut and chill. For a special treat, toast the coconut lightly on a cookie sheet at about 300° F.

PEANUT BUTTER BALLS

2 cups snipped, shredded
    coconut
½ cup peanut butter (creamy)

½ cup dried fruit, snipped*
4 tsp vanilla

Combine all ingredients and mix well. Shape into small balls between palms of hands. Arrange on waxed paper in pan and chill thoroughly. Makes 2 dozen balls.

*Dried apples, pears or apricots.

SWEET TREATS

¾ cup peanut butter
1½ cups non-fat dry milk,
    non-instant, (*or*
    1 cup dry milk and
    ½ cup whey powder)

1 cup honey
2 cups ground dried fruit, your
    choice
1 cup sunflower seeds or chopped
    nuts
coconut, optional

Rinse fruit in hot water before grinding. Mix dry milk and whey. Add peanut butter and honey and mix well. Then add fruit and seeds. Mix well. Press into buttered 9″ square pan and chill. Cut into squares.

Or mold into rolls 1½″ in diameter and roll in chopped nuts or coconut. Toasted coconut is even better. Or roll in crushed cereal flakes. Slice for serving.

HIKERS HONEY SQUARES

2 eggs
¾ cup honey
½ cup flour
 (preferably whole wheat)
¼ tsp salt

½ cup graham cracker crumbs or
 ground granola
1 cup raisins or ground cherries,
 dates, figs, or prunes
1 cup chopped nuts

Beat eggs until light and fluffy. *Gradually* add honey. If necessary, heat it slightly to pour a thin stream. Add flour, crumbs and salt. Stir in fruits and nuts. Pour in greased 8″ square baking pan. Bake at 325°-350° F. 40-45 minutes or until browned and firm in center. Cut in squares with damp knife while still warm. Cool. Makes 16 squares.

"WEIGHT-WATCHER" APPLES

(Make your own at a fraction of the cost)

Preparation: Slice apples, or cut with a French-fry potato cutter, or in strips about ¼″ thick. Spread on net on drying shelves and dry.

Or dissolve gelatin according to instructions on package (whatever flavor and color desired, red or green). Let apples soak in gelatin mixture about 10 minutes. Drain on paper towel. Place on drying rack. Makes colorful, delicious confection.

DRIED APPLE BREAD

1 cup dried apple slices
1 cup boiling water
2½ cups sifted whole wheat flour
1 tsp soda
½ tsp salt
½ cup honey
½ cup butter or margarine

2 eggs
1 tsp vanilla
1½ tbsp buttermilk
1 cup chopped nuts
3 tbsp sugar
1 tsp cinnamon
1 tbsp water

Pour boiling water over apples. Let stand 5 minutes. Pour apples and water into blender and chop. Sift flour, salt, and soda together twice. Cream butter, honey, and eggs. Add vanilla. Add chopped apple mixture, buttermilk and sifted dry ingredients. Beat. Fold in ¾ cup of the nuts. Mix sugar, cinnamon and ¼ cup of the nuts, for topping. Pour into loaf pan and sprinkle topping over mixture. Bake 50-60 minutes at 325°-350° F. Makes 1 large loaf 9¼″ × 4¾″ (inside top measure) or 2 small ones 7½″ × 3½″ (inside top measure). Bake smaller loaves about 30 minutes, or give them the toothpick test.

CHEWY APPLE COOKIES

3 cups dried apples
½ cup ground dried cherries
   or dried green grapes
1 cup boiling water
2 cups unsifted flour
   (preferably whole wheat)
⅛ tsp salt
½ tsp soda

2 tsp baking powder
½ tsp nutmeg
1 tsp. cinnamon
¼ cup margarine or butter
½ cup honey
1 egg
1 tsp vanilla
½ cup chopped nuts
½ cup coconut

Rinse apples and cherries (or grapes) so they'll go through the food grinder easily. Grind apples and cherries together. Pour boiling water over them and let stand 5 minutes.

Sift together flour, salt, soda, baking powder, nutmeg, and cinnamon. Cream butter, honey and egg. Add vanilla. Add reconstituted fruit. Add flour. Blend well. Add nuts and coconut. Drop by teaspoon onto greased cookie sheet. Bake at 350°-375° F. for 10-12 minutes. Note: Old discolored apples can be used up in this way.

DRIED APPLE CAKE OR PUDDING

3 cups dried apples
1 cup boiling water
1¼ cups unsifted flour
   (preferably whole wheat)
¼ tsp salt
1 tsp cinnamon
½ tsp nutmeg
1 tsp baking soda

¼ cup margarine or butter
½ cup brown sugar, *or*
   ⅓ cup honey
1 tsp vanilla
1 egg
½ cup chopped nuts (optional)
½ cup dried cherries or raisins
   (optional)

Rinse apples and cherries and grind in food grinder, preferably on a fine blade. Pour boiling water over fruit in a bowl and let stand 5 minutes.

Sift together 3 times, flour, salt, cinnamon, nutmeg, soda. Cream well butter and sugar. Add vanilla. Add egg and beat well. Add reconstituted dried fruit and sifted dry ingredients. Blend well. Add nuts. Pour into well-greased 8″ square pan and bake at 325°-350° F. 45-60 minutes, or until brown.

Serve hot or cold as cake *or* as pudding with the following sauce:

Sauce:

1 cup brown sugar
½ cup butter or margarine

½ cup cream or canned milk
1 tsp vanilla

Mix altogether and heat until sugar dissolves. Cut cake into squares and serve with sauce, hot or cold. Makes 9 servings. Double recipe for cake for a larger number. It's more-ish.

FRENCH APPLE PIE

Crust:

1 cup sifted flour	⅓ cup butter or margarine
¼ tsp salt	2 tbsp water

Combine salt and flour. With pastry blender cut in butter until it is a crumbly texture. Add water and work into a ball with a fork. Roll out and place in 8″ or 9″ pie pan. Bake crust at 375°-400° F. for 7 or 8 minutes or until lightly browned, or until crust is just set. *This is important to keep crust from being soggy.*

Filling:

2 cups dried apples, firmly packed	2 tbsp all-purpose flour
2 cups boiling water	½ tsp cinnamon
⅓ cup sugar	1 tbsp butter

Pour boiling water over dried apples and let stand 5 minutes. Simmer until apples are tender while mixing crust. Mix sugar, flour, cinnamon together and add to apples. Continue cooking until thickened, stirring to keep from scorching. Pour apple mixture into pre-baked pie shell and dot with butter.

Topping:

¼ cup butter or margarine	½ cup all-purpose flour
⅓ cup brown sugar	

Mix altogether until crumbly and sprinkle over apple mixture. Bake pie at 350° F. about 55 minutes or until browned. Serve hot or cold, plain or with cheese, whipped cream, or ice cream. This is especially good made with stoneground whole wheat flour instead of all-purpose flour.

APRICOT SNOWBALLS

48 dried apricot halves	2 tsp orange juice
1½ cups shredded coconut	2 tbsp powdered sugar

Wash apricots. Put through food grinder together with coconut. Blend in juice and powdered sugar, shape into ¾″ balls, and roll in date sugar. (Turbinado sugar or fructose may be substituted for date sugar.)

DRIED APPLE TURNOVERS

2 cups dried apples
1½ cups boiling water
¼ cup sugar or honey*

2 tbsp butter or margarine
1 tsp cinnamon
Pastry for 2 9″ pie shells

Pour boiling water over dried apples and let stand 5 minutes. Simmer until tender. Water should be almost completely absorbed. Add honey, butter, and cinnamon to apples.

Roll pastry into oblong, not too thin. Cut into 12 4″ or 5″ squares. Divide apple mixture, spooning onto half of each square. Press edges together securely. Fry in deep fat at 375° F. for about 4 minutes or until golden brown on both sides. Or bake at 350°-375° F. for 20 minutes.

*If you have a very sweet tooth, you may want to increase honey to ½ cup.

DRIED APRICOT BREAD*

1 cup dried apricots
2 cups sifted whole wheat flour
3 tsp baking powder
¼ tsp salt
1 cup brown sugar

4 tbsp soft butter or margarine
2 eggs, beaten
¼ cup orange juice
½ cup chopped nuts

Barely cover apricots with boiling water and let stand 5 minutes. Drain and snip coarsely. Sift together the flour, baking powder and salt. Cream sugar and butter. Add beaten egg. Add dry ingredients alternately with orange juice. Fold in chopped nuts and apricots. Bake in well-greased, floured loaf pan 50-55 minutes at 325°-350° F.

Note: This is one way to use up those old darkened apricots.

*(Recipe from *Wheat for Man, Why and How,* by Rosenvall, Miller & Flack.)

APRICOT-COCONUT COOKIES

2 cups dried apricots
1 (14-oz.) can Eagle Brand milk
2 cups shredded coconut

1 tbsp orange juice
½ cup slivered blanched almonds
2 cups shredded coconut, for
    coating

Snip apricots with scissors into rather small pieces. Place in a sieve and put under running water. Drain. Leave apricot pieces in sieve and place over boiling water to soften. Combine all ingredients. Drop by teaspoon onto pile of coconut on waxed paper. Coat. Place balls on well-greased cookie sheets. Bake in slow oven 275°-300° F. for 30-35 minutes. Do not overbake. With spatula remove from pans immediately. If they collapse a bit or stick, mold together with hands and they will hold together as they cool. Makes about 5 dozen.

BANANA COOKIES

1 cup dried bananas
1 cup boiling water
1¾ cups sifted flour
   (whole wheat preferred)
2 tsp baking powder
½ tsp salt
½ tsp nutmeg

½ cup butter or margarine
1 cup brown sugar
1 egg, beaten
1 tsp vanilla
1½ cups quick-cooking oatmeal
½ cup chopped nuts, optional

Pour boiling water over bananas and let stand at least 5-10 minutes. Sift together twice flour, baking powder, salt, and nutmeg. Cream butter and sugar. Add vanilla. Cream in beaten egg. Whirl bananas in blender until thoroughly mashed. Add banana with sifted dry ingredients. Add oatmeal and nuts and blend well.

Drop by teaspoon onto greased cookie sheet. Bake 12-15 minutes at 350°-375° F. or until lightly browned. Makes about 4 dozen.

BANANA NUT LOAF

1 cup dried bananas, packed well
1 cup boiling water
2 cups sifted flour
   (preferably whole wheat)
¼ tsp salt

2 tbsp sour milk
1 tsp soda
2 eggs, separated
¼ cup butter
1 cup chopped nuts

Pour boiling water over dried bananas and let stand 5 minutes. Whirl in blender. Beat egg whites. Cream together egg yolks, pureed bananas, sugar, butter. Dissolve soda in sour milk and add to creamed mixture along with flour. Blend well. Fold in beaten egg whites and nuts. Bake in greased and floured loaf pan about 45 minutes at 350°-375° F. or until inserted toothpick comes out clean.

BANANA COCONUT BARS

2½ cups sifted flour
   (preferably whole wheat)
1 tsp baking powder
¼ tsp salt
1 cup dried bananas
¾ cup boiling water

½ cup butter or margarine
1 cup brown sugar
1 tsp vanilla
2 eggs
½ cup chopped nuts

Pour boiling water over dried bananas and let stand 5 minutes. Sift together flour, baking powder, salt. Cream butter, sugar, vanilla and eggs. Whirl bananas in blender. Add puree to creamed mixture. Add flour. Blend. Fold in nuts last. Pour into greased 9″ × 13″ pan and bake at 300°-325° F. about 45 minutes. Cool slightly and glaze with thin powdered sugar icing. Sprinkle with coconut. Cut into bars.

ORANGE DRIED-PEAR BARS

1 cup chopped dried pears
½ cup boiling water
1 tsp grated dried orange peel
  (1 tbsp if fresh)
1 cup flour
  (whole wheat preferred)
½ tsp baking powder

¾ tsp soda
¼ cup butter or margarine
½ cup brown sugar
1 tsp almond extract
¼ cup milk
¼ cup orange juice

Pour boiling water over pears and orange peel and let stand 5 minutes. Cream butter, brown sugar, and egg. Add almond flavoring. Add dry ingredients alternately with milk, orange juice and pears. Blend well. Pour into greased 8″ square pan. Bake 25-30 minutes at 325°-350° F. or until lightly browned. Cool. Cut into 16 squares.

PLUM PUFFS

1 cup dried plums
1 cup boiling water
½ tbsp dried orange rind
3 cups unsifted flour
4 tsp baking powder
¼ tsp salt
½ tsp nutmeg

½ tsp cinnamon
4 eggs, beaten
¾ cup brown sugar
1 cup milk
¾ cup sugar
1 tsp cinnamon

Mix plums and orange rind, then pour boiling water over them. Let stand at least 5 minutes, while mixing other ingredients. Sift together twice flour, baking powder, salt, nutmeg, cinnamon. Beat eggs well. Add sugar and beat until thick and lemony. Add milk and sifted dry ingredients alternately. Drain plums and fold into batter. Drop by teaspoons into hot oil and deep fry until golden brown. Set browned puffs on paper towel. Mix ¾ cup sugar and the cinnamon in a shallow bowl. Roll hot fried puffs in mixture. Makes about 4 dozen.

OLD-FASHIONED PLUM PUDDING

½ lb. finely chopped suet
½ lb. raisins or cherries
½ lb. currants
½ lb. golden raisins (green
  seedless grapes, dried)
½ lb. dried plums, snipped
1½ cups sifted whole wheat flour
½ tsp allspice
½ tsp cinnamon
½ tsp nutmeg
¼ tsp cloves

¼ tsp ginger
¼ tsp mace
½ tsp salt
1 tsp baking powder
1½ cups bread crumbs
1½ cups brown sugar
4 eggs, well beaten
½ cup molasses
¼ cup apricot nectar or apple juice
½ cup chopped nuts

68

Drying Fruit

Combine suet and prepared fruit. Sift in a little of the flour and toss to blend. With remaining flour, sift spices, baking powder, and salt. Stir into fruit along with bread crumbs and brown sugar. Beat eggs and combine with molasses and fruit juice. Stir into fruit and flour mixture until well blended. Add nuts.

Spoon batter into two 1-quart molds, or the equivalent, which have been well greased. Cover with double thickness of foil. Set them on a rack in large kettle. Add boiling water halfway up the side. Cover kettle and steam 3 hours. Serve hot with desired sauce. Serves 15.

Pudding may be made weeks ahead and stored in a cool place, or frozen. Reheat by steaming 1 hour.

DRIED RHUBARB BREAD

1 cup dried rhubarb	1 egg
½ cup boiling water	1 cup sour cream
2½ cups unsifted flour	1 tsp vanilla
1 tsp salt	½ cup chopped nuts
1 tsp soda	½ cup granulated sugar
1 cup brown sugar	1 tbsp softened butter
2/3 cup oil	

Pour boiling water over rhubarb and let stand 5 minutes. Cook about 15 minutes. Add a little more water if necessary to keep from scorching. Cream brown sugar, oil and egg. Beat well. Add vanilla. Add sour cream with sifted dry ingredients, blending well for a smooth consistency. Stir in rhubarb and chopped nuts.

Pour into 2 greased loaf pans. Combine granulated sugar and butter. Sprinkle over top of batter. Bake at 325°-350° F. for 60 minutes or until done. Set a piece of foil lightly on top for the first half hour of baking time, so rhubarb bits on top will not get brittle. Remove for browning during last half of baking.

RHUBARB SLUSH

1½ cups dried rhubarb, preferably red variety	1 cup sugar
1½ cups boiling water	Chilled carbonated beverage

Pour boiling water over dried rhubarb. Let stand 5 minutes. Add ½ cup more water and boil slowly until rhubarb is tender. Add sugar. Stir and let cook 5 minutes more. Drain in colander. Press, but not much pulp will come through. Put juice in ice tray to freeze. Spoon slush into punch cups about two-thirds full. Pour beverage over slush and serve.

RHUBARB-STRAWBERRY DESSERT OR SALAD

½ cup dried rhubarb
3 cups boiling water
1 cup dried strawberry slices *or*
  1 10-oz. pkg. frozen strawberries (sweetened)*

¾ to 1 cup sugar (to suit your
  taste)
1 6-oz. pkg. strawberry gelatin
1 cup whipping cream

Pour boiling water over combined rhubarb and strawberries. Let stand 5 minutes. Boil or simmer about 15 minutes until quite tender. Add a little more water if necessary to keep from scorching. Drain in a colander set in a bowl. Measure drained liquid and add enough water to make 1 cup. Bring to a full boil and pour over gelatin, stirring to dissolve. Set in refrigerator. When partially set, but not solid, whip cream. Fold cream into gelatin, then gently fold in drained fruit. Chill several hours. Spoon into sherbet dishes and top with granola, if serving for dessert.

If serving for salad, follow above instructions, but add 1 tbsp unflavored gelatin to strawberry gelatin to increase firmness. Fold in 1 cup cottage cheese with fruit and ½ to 1 cup chopped nuts or sunflower seeds. Chill in a mold and serve on lettuce. Makes 8 to 10 servings.

*If using sweetened frozen strawberries, eliminate the sugar which is listed in the recipe.

SPRING SHORTCAKE

1 cup dried rhubarb bits
1 cup boiling water

1 cup sugar
2 cups fresh strawberries*

Pour boiling water over rhubarb and let stand 5 minutes. Simmer rhubarb about 20 to 30 minutes until tender, adding more water to keep from sticking or scorching. Stir occasionally. Add sugar and cook a few minutes longer. Combine strawberries and hot rhubarb sauce. Chill. Serve over shortcakes and top with whipped cream.

*Dried strawberries may be used instead of fresh. Use 1 cup of dried strawberries and 1 cup of boiling water and cook rhubarb and strawberries together, stirring very carefully, so fruit is not mashed. If dried strawberries are used, cut sugar in half.

DRIED RHUBARB PIE

1½ cups boiling water
1½ cups dried rhubarb bits
2 eggs
1 cup sugar

2 tsp vanilla
1½ tbsp melted butter
3 tbsp flour

Drying Fruit

Pour boiling water over rhubarb and let stand 5 minutes. Cook, stirring occasionally, 15-20 minutes on low heat, until rhubarb is quite tender. Add a little more water, if necessary, to keep rhubarb from sticking or scorching.

Roll out your favorite pie crust in a 9″ pie pan.

Beat eggs. Add sugar, flour, vanilla and melted butter. Beat about 5 minutes. Fold in cooked rhubarb. Place in uncooked pie shell. Bake 10 minutes at 400° F. Place a sheet of foil to keep top and crust from browning too much. Reduce heat to 300°-325° F. and bake about 35 minutes longer, or until done. Remove foil last 15 minutes. Cool and top with whipped cream or sprinkle with granola.

Try apricots with this recipe. Snip into small pieces with the scissors and follow same directions.

DRIED APRICOT COOKIES

(Other brittle dried fruits may be used, according to preference.)

2¼ cups sifted whole wheat flour	1 cup soft butter
½ tsp soda	1 cup brown sugar, packed
1 tsp salt	2 eggs
½-¾ cup dried apricot powder and bits*	2 tsp vanilla

Sift together flour, soda, salt. Whirl dried fruit in blender until it is a combination of powder and bits. Cream butter, sugar, eggs. Add vanilla. Beat well. Add sifted dry ingredients and beat until smooth. Add fruit. Chill, if time permits. Drop by rounded teaspoons onto a greased cookie sheet 2″ apart. Bake at 350°-375° F. until lightly browned, 8-10 minutes. Do not overbake because fruit bits may harden. Cool slightly, then remove from cookie sheet. If properly stored, fruit bits will remain soft and chewy. Makes about 6 dozen cookies.

*If soft apricots are all you have, snip in small bits with scissors. The value of this recipe is that you can use up those brittle fruits, especially if your apricots turned dark or have black spots.

PREPARING AND DRYING FRUITS

This drying chart gives *suggested guidelines*. Other procedures may be more successful for your particular locality and climate. Because humidity, heat, and food itself are all variable considerations, there is no way to be specific on drying times. Even dehydrators and ovens vary greatly in efficiency. Keep your own time notes so you can profit by your experience for succeeding years. Preparation of food dictates variable drying time, e.g., leaving pitted cherries whole or in half, peaches or pears in slices, halves, or quarters, etc. See chapter 3, Pretreatment, on variations of dips and "gilding the lily." "Bisulfite" means to dip in sodium bisulfite or ascorbic acid solution. Keep heat under 145° F. for better retention of nutrients.

Fruit and prime condition	Preparation and Pretreatment*	Drying Procedure	Dryness Test
Apples Most varieties, Jonathan, Golden & Red Delicious, Rome Beauty are favorites. Mature but not soft.	Wash, core & peel if necessary. Cut into ¼" slices or rings, or grate or chop. Steam or blanch 10 min. Or sulfur 30 min. Or Bisulfite 2 min. Drain. Or no pretreatment necessary.	Spread in single layer on net on drying rack.	Leathery, suede-like, no moisture when cut and squeezed.
Apricots Use any variety. Fully ripened. Leather those too soft.	Wash, halve and pit. Sulfur 1 to 2 hours, depending on size. Or Bisulfite 2 min. Or steam 5-10 min. Or "pop backs" and dry without pretreatment.	Arrange pit side up in single layer on net-covered drying shelf. Turn over after several hours to speed drying.	Leathery, pliable. No moisture in center when cut. Takes 2 to 3 days with "popped" backs.

Fruit and prime condition	Preparation and Pretreatment	Drying Procedure	Dryness Test
Avocado Ripe when slightly soft and skin peels off easily.	Peel, pit and slice ¼" thick. Bisulfite 2 min. Drain.	Arrange in single layer on drying shelf.	Leathery, pliable.
Bananas Ripe or overripe after starch has been converted to natural sugar. Brown dots or brown skin, but not mushy.	Peel. Slice in rounds or lengthwise. Bisulfite 2 min. Drain. Or no pretreatment.	Arrange in single layer on net on drying shelf. Turn over to speed drying.	Leathery to brittle.
Blueberries, blackberries, loganberries, cranberries, huckleberries, gooseberries (pink when ripe)	Sort, wash, stem where necessary Steam or blanch 2 min. to crack skins. Dip in cold water. Drain.	Arrange on net on drying shelf in single layer. Scatter to turn as they dry.	Leathery to brittle.

*See Chapter 3 on Pretreatment, pp. 23-28.

Fruit and prime condition	Preparation and Pretreatment*	Drying Procedure	Dryness Test
Raspberries, dewberries, mulberries	Sort, wash, stem. Steam 15-30 seconds. Dip in cold water. Or Bisulfite 2 min. Drain. Enhances color. Or no pretreatment.	Arrange on net on drying shelf in single layer. Scatter to turn as they dry.	Leathery to brittle.
Cantaloupes (& Muskmelon & Honey Dew)	Peel. Cut into ¼"-½" slices. Bisulfite 2 minutes. Drain. Or no pretreatment.	Arrange on net on drying shelf in single layer. Turn after a few hours.	Leathery to brittle.
Cherries Any variety, including pie. Firm but not overripe.	Sort, wash, stem, pit. Crack skins by steaming or blanching 1-2 minutes. Drain. Or no pretreatment. Steaming speeds drying and helps to preserve color.	Arrange on net on drying shelf in single layer. Turn after a few hours. Drippy. Stick badly.	Leathery, slightly sticky, like raisins. Takes 2 to 4 days. Loses luster.
Citrus Fruits: Grapefruit Lemons Limes Kumquats Oranges Tangerines	Peel fruit and separate sections. Bisulfite 10 min. Drain. Prick holes in sections with fork to speed drying. Or no pretreatment. Do not dry in sun. Steam peels at least 10 min. Bisulfite added to steaming water enhances color. Drain. Or freeze peels and grate. Use in recipes calling for these products.	Arrange sections on net on drying rack, to catch drips. Turn after a few hours. Arrange on drying rack Spread evenly on plastic wrap to catch small particles.	No moisture when squeezed. Leathery to brittle Dry and brittle

Fruit and prime condition	Preparation and Pretreatment*	Drying Procedure	Dryness Test
Dates With low moisture content. Pick translucent fruit.	Wipe clean with damp terry towel. Do not wash. Discard fruit with fungus, damaged skin or souring. Dry one type of date at a time in the same batch. No pretreatment necessary.	Spread on dryer rack in single layer. Turn as needed to speed drying. Pasteurize sundried dates. (See chapter 5 on storing)	Leathery, pliable, slightly sticky. Takes 2 to 8 days. Temperature above 155° F. causes sugars to caramelize and taste scorched.
Figs Leave on trees until ripe enough to fall to ground. Immature figs become woody, with poor flavor. Sugar content is too low.	Wash. Leave whole if small, or cut in half lengthwise. Crack skins by dipping in boiling water 15-45 seconds, then in cold water. Drain. Blot dry. Or sulfur 1 hour. Or no pretreatment. Or chop, if desired.	Spread on net on drying rack. Stir or turn after a few hours, to speed drying and keep from sticking. May be sun dried.	Leathery, pliable, slightly sticky. Takes 1 to 3 days.
Grapes Seedless (green) Black Ribbier or Tokay	Wash & remove defective fruit. Remove from stems. Crack skins by steaming or blanching 15-30 seconds, then dip in cold water. Drain. Or slash skin.	Spread in single layer on net on dryer shelf.	Leathery, like raisins.
Fruit Mix Your choice of pears, peaches, apples, figs, dates, plums, grapes, etc.	Cube or reduce to small chunks, or chop different kinds separately. Steam or blanch 15-30 seconds. Drain. Blot dry. Or no pretreatment.	Spread in single layer on net or plastic wrap to catch small bits. Stir to speed drying.	Leathery to brittle.

*See Chapter 3 on Pretreatment, pp. 23-28.

Fruit and prime condition	Preparation and Pretreatment*	Drying Procedure	Dryness Test
Guava (lemon guava)	Wash. Do not peel. Remove seeds & center pulp. Quarter, or slice even smaller.	Arrange on net on drying rack. Turn, to speed drying.	Leathery.
Papaya Fully ripened.	Peel, remove seeds, slice ¼" thick. Bisulfite 2 min. Drain.	Arrange on net on drying rack. Turn, to speed drying.	Leathery.
Nectarines	Prepare according to directions for peaches.		
Peaches Use any freestone variety. Ripe, but not dead-ripe.	Peel. Halve and pit. Quarter or slice ¼"-½". Sulfur halves 2 hours. Or steam 15-18 min. Or Bisulfite 2 min. Drain. Or no pretreatment.	Arrange slices or halves on net on drying rack. Turn, to speed drying. Overripe spots may go black.	Leathery to brittle.
Pears Bartlett preferred.	Peel or not. Cut in half lengthwise and core. Quarter or slice ¼" to ½". Bisulfite 2 min. Or sulfur 1 hour. Or no pretreatment.	Arrange in single layer on net on drying rack. Turn, to speed drying.	Leathery, suede-like. No moisture when cut.
Persimmons Dry only ripe fruit. Unripe is bitter.	Peel. Cut in half or slice. Steam 15-18 minutes or Bisulfite 2 min. This removes tendency to pucker the mouth. Drain.	Arrange in single layer on net on drying rack. Turn, to speed drying.	Leathery. No moisture when cut.

Fruit and prime condition	Preparation and Pretreatment	Drying Procedure	Dryness Test
Pineapple Ripe but firm. Orange in color, not green. If soft, flesh will be dark in spots.	Cut in half, then wedges about 1½"-2", depending on size of whole fruit. Trim away core. Peel. Remove eyes. Place on plate (not cutting board because of excess juice) and cut into ½"-¼" slices or bits. Bisulfite 2 min. Or no pretreatment.	Arrange in single layer on drying rack, on net, to catch drips. Turn, to speed drying. Keep temperature under 130° F. Scorches easily.	Leathery.
Plums-Prunes All kinds. Mature, but use over-ripe fruit for leather.	Wash. Cut in half and pit. Pop back of small plums, like apricots. Slice larger fruit. Steam or blanch 30 sec. to crack skins. Or steam halves 15 min., slices 5. Or sulfur whole fruit 2 hours, halves and slices 1 hour. Or no pretreatment.	Arrange on net on dry-ing rack. Turn, to speed drying.	Pliable, leathery.
Rhubarb Red variety preferred.	Wash. Slice crosswise ½". Steam 2-4 minutes only. Drain.	Spread pieces on net on drying rack. Stir to speed drying.	Brittle.
Watermelon	One way to use that leftover melon. Slice ¼"-½". Remove seeds. Steam or Bisulfite 2 min. Or no pretreatment.	Arrange on net on drying rack. Turn, to speed drying.	Leathery. Will scorch easily.

*See Chapter 3 on Pretreatment, pp. 23-28.

Chapter 8
DRYING VEGETABLES AND HERBS

Vegetables

Vegetables are not home-dried as a popular storage item. But you may be surprised to learn how adaptable they really are and how easily they can be used in your own recipes. Although fruits are delicious snacks, vegetables are less so. However, carrots, which contain considerable sugar, are good snack food.

Since we are primarily concerned with saving food and money, drying vegetables does deserve consideration, but with an eye to sensible economy. For example, why take precious time and energy to dry vegetables that are readily available the year around? It's a good idea to have them on hand for emergency. But if you have to buy carrots in the market, you won't experience any savings in money, unless you get a real "buy" on them. Also, such food has diminished in quality because of transportation time and then simply deteriorating at room temperature on the produce counter for who knows how long? To further diminish nutrients by the process of drying and then reconstituting for consumption is waste, not economy.

If, on the other hand, produce is harvested from your own garden and prepared for the dryer immediately, you have achieved a saving of nutrition as well as money. (See Carrots under Convenience Foods in chapter 1.) So it makes "cents" to use your head in deciding what should be dried.

Drying small amounts of several excess vegetables or fruits can usually be done at the same time to avoid waste of food and conserve energy use of dehydrator or oven.

Vegetables should be in prime condition at the time of preparation. All vegetables contain enzymes the same as fruits. The enzymes speed up their ripening action at the time of picking, affecting the color, flavor, texture, sugar content and nutrients. Harvest vegetables as early in the day as possible, while they are still cool. Then prepare them for the dehydrator as quickly as possible to preserve food value.

Because vegetables are low-acid, most of them should be blanched or steamed to preserve vitamins, color, flavor and to speed drying. Such pretreatment also ensures better storage. When reconstituted, they have better color and require less presoaking and cooking time than unblanched vegetables.

To test for doneness in drying vegetables, remove a few pieces from the drying rack and let them cool thoroughly. Warm food always feels softer and more moist. Check charts for desired condition. Most vegetables should be brittle. Store in airtight containers or seal in heavy plastic bags.

A dehydrator or oven is especially preferred for drying vegetables, because once the drying process has started, it should continue without interruption. Molds can grow on partly dried foods at room temperature and molds might produce harmful or toxic effects.

Beans and peas can be left on the vine to mature. After picking the pods, drop them into a bag of loosely-woven material, such as cheesecloth or burlap. Tie the bag and suspend it in the sunshine for several days. Always bring the bag in at night to protect from dew or moisture. When beans and peas are thoroughly dry, beat the bag with a heavy stick to release the contents from the hulls. Separate the food from the residue. To protect from insect infestation before storing, heat them in a preheated oven 165° F. for 30 minutes. *Cool,* then place in airtight containers.

Herbs

Herbs are used in many ways: medicinal purposes, herb teas, perfumes, sachets, and for seasoning foods.

An herb is a low-growing plant with juicy stems when young. Older stems have hard, woody tissues. Herbs are generally perennial, dying each year and returning the following season. Most herbs can be dried and used for healthful teas or to delicately flavor foods. They retain their fresh flavor up to six months or longer, if kept in a dry, dark, cool spot.

Herb and spice shelves should not be kept near the stove or the refrigerator, and should be kept dark. Heat from cooking diminishes flavors as does the heat diffused from the outside of the refrigerator. If a dark cabinet is not available, store the herbs in tinted jars or wrap the jars in decorative dark paper. Label and date herbs as they are purchased, so you can keep track of the freshness. When in doubt, smell. If the odor is dusty with only a faint aroma, it won't do much good to add as flavoring or seasoning to food.

During the summer some fruit stands sell such herbs as basil, mint, chives, sage, and thyme. Potted herbs can be purchased at green-houses. You can plant them in your garden or keep them growing on the windowsill for a constant fresh supply.

They can be chopped and frozen, wrapped in small plastic bags and used as needed.

You may tie a small bunch of herbs together and suspend from a line

80

inside the house. Do not dry them in the direct sun. Or you may dry them in the oven or dehydrator.

For oven drying, wash leaves gently and blot dry. Place on oven drying rack and dry at the lowest possible heat with oven door ajar. Herbs require an even lower temperature than fruit or vegetables. Dry until crisp, but don't overdry.

For the dehydrator, spread the washed leaves on the shelves and dry preferably about 110°-120° F.

Store carefully in plastic bags in a cool, dark, dry place. Herbs will keep their flavor longer if kept in a leaf state rather than chopped, crumbled, or ground.

Dried herbs can be ground or powdered for seasoning entrées and casseroles. They can be crumbled and sprinkled on salads for extra nutrition and flavor. They make delicious healthful teas, using about a teaspoon of crumbled leaves per cup of boiling water. Let steep five to ten minutes. Honey enhances the flavor. Also a little lemon juice is a good addition.

Best-known herbs are chervil, chives, comfrey, fennel, lavender, marjoram, mint, rosemary, sage, saffron, spearmint, tansy, tarragon, thyme.

Many books have been written on herbs and their use, among them *The Herbalist* by Joseph H. Meyer (Clarence Meyer, 9th printing, 1972).

For suggestions on the preparation and drying of vegetables, see also the charts at the end of this chapter.

General Suggestions for Vegetables

Most vegetables should be reconstituted by pouring an equal amount of boiling water over dried food in a bowl. Let stand five minutes. Then simmer longer in the unabsorbed water until tender. Add water as needed to keep from scorching.

For high altitudes, blanching or steaming time is slightly longer than what is given. Try the time prescribed and see how it looks, then steam longer, if necessary.

Potatoes must be par-cooked or they will turn almost black during drying. Steam or blanch until they are translucent. Use as dip chips. They can be reconstituted for use in recipes, but will retain some of the leatheriness.

When the word "reconstitute" appears, it means to pour an equal amount of boiling water over vegetables in a bowl, then let them stand five minutes.

Dried beets can be reconstituted, then simmered until tender. Use barely enough water to prevent scorching.

Make a sauce of orange juice. Thicken with cornstarch and flavor with brown sugar or honey if needed. Add canned mandarin orange sections. Pour over hot beets and serve.

Dried carrots are versatile in stews and soups. Reconstitute for tenderness and shorter simmering. Grated dried carrots are ready for reconstituting in boiling water, to be used in salads (chill in refrigerator for more crispness), cookies and cakes, or to be dropped in soups.

Slice carrots thin and marinate in barbeque sauce and dry. Delicious as snacks or dip chips.

Greens (chard, beet greens, spinach, etc.) are rich in vitamin C. To prevent deterioration and loss of crispness, they should be washed and prepared for the dryer immediately after picking.

To prepare, float leaves in plenty of cold water and wash gently, so leaves are not damaged. If stems are large and heavy, cut them out with sharp tip of paring knife for quick drying, because stems dry slowly. Stems can be cut out before or after steaming, whichever you prefer. Steam only two to four minutes, so leaves don't mat or mush. Arrange carefully on drying rack. Don't pile together. Dry on low heat, not over 125° F. Will dry in two or three hours. Lift brittle leaves carefully into storage container, preferably heavy plastic bags. Arranging one thickness on racks speeds drying. If you have more than the dryer can accommodate all at once, refrigerate unused greens and put in a second batch as quickly as possible.

To reconstitute, pour boiling water over leaves, barely enough to cover. Let stand five minutes, then simmer a few minutes until tender. Do not salt until serving time, and then only sparingly. The greens will probably absorb all the moisture, so watch carefully to prevent scorching. Serve with a little lemon juice on top.

Dried onions are also a versatile vegetable. Onions can be sliced, chopped or cubed, according to the intended use. Reconstitute before using. Chopped or cubed, onions can be dropped in soups and stews.

Reconstituted onion slices can be deep fried.

Onion slices can be reconstituted and used with dissolved bouillon cubes for French Onion Soup.

Dried squash or *pumpkin* wears many faces.

Banana or hubbard squash can be reconstituted and used as a mashed vegetable, seasoned with salt and butter, or it can be used in recipes.

Drying Vegetables and Herbs

Pumpkin can be reconstituted and used in your favorite pumpkin chiffon pie recipe, or in pumpkin bread and cookies.

Zucchini is so plentiful we need many ways to use it. Slice thin and use as dip chips. Marinate in barbeque sauce for variety.

It can be sliced, dried and reconstituted for use in recipes calling for sliced zucchini. Remember that it will be somewhat leathery and not crisp.

It can be grated and dried, then reconstituted to be used for zucchini bread, cookies, cakes, and casseroles.

Dried tomatoes also have a variety of uses.

Fresh tomatoes can be boiled to a pulp and put through a sieve to remove seeds and use as puree for leather. The leather can be eaten as snacks or can be dropped in soup for flavoring.

Or slice thin before drying and use as dip chips.

Or drop slices in blender and powder for flavoring or for making tomato sauce for casseroles and other recipes. (See Recipes.)

Or drop slices in soups.

Or drop slices in blender to make flakes and sprinkle over salads for color and nutrition.

Recipes

See Chapter 10 for instructions in making ground gluten and TVP granules for use in many main dishes.

BURGER SOUP

½ cup sliced dried carrots
½ cup dried corn
¼ cup dried onion
3 cups boiling water
2 cups ground gluten* or TVP
  granules
⅛ tsp oregano

⅛ tsp basil
½ tsp seasoned salt
¼ cup dried tomatoes, powdered
2 cups diced potatoes
1 cup sliced celery
1 tbsp soy sauce

Pour all the boiling water over combined dried onion, carrots, and corn. Let stand 5 minutes. Then simmer in large pan and add all ingredients, except gluten, until vegetables are tender (about 1 hour). About halfway through the cooking, add gluten or TVP.

This soup may be cooked in a crockpot, as follows: Heat crockpot. Add boiling water and drop in all ingredients, except gluten or TVP. Cook on low heat for 6 to 8 hours. Add gluten or TVP last part of cooking. Makes about 6 servings.

*Brown ground gluten in a little olive oil. Dissolve 2 beef-flavored bouillon cubes in a little hot water and add to browned gluten. Let simmer a few minutes and then add to soup.

COLESLAW

1 cup dried cabbage   1½-2 cups boiling water

Pour boiling water over cabbage. Let stand 5 minutes. Then put in refrigerator in tightly covered container. Chill 1 to 2 hours.

Dressing:

½ cup mayonnaise or salad   2 tbsp vinegar
  dressing   1 tsp mustard

Combine dressing with cabbage and serve. Sprinkle sesame seeds into salad for extra flavor and nutrition.

DRIED CABBAGE CASSEROLE

2 cups dried shredded cabbage   ½ cup grated cheese
2 cups boiling water   Bacon bits (TVP)
2 cups white sauce

Pour boiling water over cabbage. Let stand 5 minutes, then cook on medium or low heat about 15 minutes. Cabbage will not be quite as tender as fresh cabbage. Water will be absorbed. Careful, don't burn. Make white sauce. Put cooked cabbage in greased casserole. Pour medium white sauce over it. Top with grated cheese. Bake 15-20 minutes at 300°-325° F. Remove from oven and sprinkle bacon bits on top. Makes 4-6 servings.

WHITE SAUCE

Thin:

1 cup milk   1 tbsp butter or margarine
1 tbsp all-purpose flour   ¼ tsp salt

Medium:

1 cup milk   2 tbsp butter or margarine
2 tbsp all-purpose flour   ¼ tsp salt

Thick:

1 cup milk   2 tbsp butter or margarine
3 tbsp all-purpose flour   ¼ tsp salt

Melt butter in frying pan. Add flour and salt. Stir until smooth. Pour in cold liquid, stirring constantly to prevent lumping. Boil 2 minutes.

DRIED STRING BEANS

2 cups dried string beans
2 cups boiling water

Bacon bits (TVP)
Salt to taste

Pour boiling water over beans in a pan. Let stand 5 minutes. Simmer until tender and water is almost absorbed. When tender, add salt as needed. Sprinkle with bacon bits. Serve hot.

DRIED BEAN-BURGER CASSEROLE

1½ cups dried string beans
1½ cups boiling water
2 cups ground gluten or TVP
Salt to taste

About 2 cups mashed potatoes
  (instant potatoes can be used)
1 can tomato soup*
1 cup grated cheese

Pour boiling water over string beans and let stand 5 minutes. Simmer unsalted until tender. Add ground gluten or TVP to tomato soup and let stand to absorb flavor. Put reconstituted green beans in greased baking dish (about 2-quart). Pour gluten-soup mixture over beans. Spoon mashed potatoes on top. Sprinkle grated cheese on top. Bake at 325°-350° F. 20 to 30 minutes or until cheese melts well. Makes 4-6 servings.
*Make your own tomato sauce for this recipe by whirling a dozen large tomato slices in the blender until powdered. Cook this powder with 1½ cups water. Add a little dried onion, if desired.

FAST HASH

1 cup ground gluten or TVP
1 tsp instant beef-flavored bouillon
  or 2 beef-flavor bouillon cubes
1 cup hot water
1 large egg, beaten
1 tbsp dried milk

½ tsp salt, more or less to
  taste preference
3 tbsp minced onion
2 tbsp whole wheat flour
¼ tsp sugar
1 pkg frozen hash brown potatoes

Pour hot water over gluten and bouillon. If using cubes, dissolve in hot water first. Let stand 15 minutes. Combine all ingredients, except potatoes. Brown slightly in oil in frying pan. Add potatoes and cook until done. Add a little water while cooking to prevent sticking. Season more if necessary.

CARROT SALAD

1 cup dried grated carrots
½ cup dried pineapple chunks
½ cup dried ground cherries

2 cups boiling water
Mayonnaise
Mini marshmallows, optional

Pour boiling water over dried carrots and fruit. Let stand 5 minutes. Chill. Add mayonnaise to suit your taste. Mix together well and serve on lettuce or bed of sprouted grain. Chewy and filling.

DRIED GRATED-CARROT COOKIES

1 cup dried grated carrots
2 tsp dried grated orange rind
¾ cup boiling water
2 cups sifted flour
1 tsp baking powder
½ tsp soda
¼ tsp salt

1 cup brown sugar
1 cup butter or margarine
1 tsp vanilla
1 egg, beaten
1 cup coconut, optional
1 cup dried cherries, ground
1 cup chopped nuts, optional

Pour boiling water over carrots and orange rind. Sift together flour, baking powder, soda, salt. Cream brown sugar and margarine. Add vanilla. Add beaten egg and beat well. Add dry ingredients with carrot mixture. Stir well and fold in coconut, cherries and nuts. Drop by teaspoons on greased cookie sheet and bake 10-15 minutes at 350°-375° F.

CARROT CAKE

1½ cups grated dried carrots
1½ cups boiling water
3¾ cups sifted whole wheat flour
2 tsp soda
2 tsp cinnamon
½ tsp allspice
½ tsp nutmeg
½ tsp cloves

1 tsp salt
1 cup honey
¾ cup oil
4 eggs, well beaten
1 cup canned crushed pineapple,
  drained
1 tsp vanilla
1 cup nuts

Pour boiling water over grated carrots. Let stand 5 minutes. Sift dry ingredients together twice. Cream honey, oil, and eggs. Add pineapple and carrots, including water which may not be absorbed, then dry ingredients and vanilla. Mix well. Fold in nuts. Bake in greased and floured 9″ × 13″ pan or well-greased and floured Bundt pan 30-45 minutes at 325°-350° F.

CREAM CHEESE ICING

8-oz pkg soft cream cheese
2 cups powdered sugar
1 cup flaked coconut

¼ cup margarine
2 tsp vanilla
½ cup chopped pecans

Beat cream cheese, margarine, sugar and vanilla. Blend in coconut and pecans and spread over cooled cake.

DRIED CORN
(Served as a vegetable)
2 cups dried corn serves about 8 when reconstituted.

Dried corn can be reconstituted by combining equal parts of boiling water and corn. Let stand 5 minutes. Then simmer about 15 minutes until tender. Add more water if necessary to prevent scorching.

Never add salt until tender and then only if necessary. Serve with butter.

For Creamed Dried Corn (a special taste treat), prepare as above. When tender pour milk over the cooked corn. Add a tablespoon of butter. Heat. Stir in thickening made from a little flour or cornstarch and water, shaken in a closed jar until smooth. Cook until milk is thickened. Add salt to taste.

Cook dried corn as in first paragraph above. Then add light cream (half and half) and heat before serving. Season as desired with salt and a little brown sugar.

CORN PANCAKES

3 eggs, separated
½ cup dried corn, ground fine in
  a wheat grinder
½ tsp salt
1 tsp baking powder

1½ cups whole wheat flour
1¾ cups milk
¼ cup oil
¼ cup honey

Beat egg whites stiff. Sift corn flour, whole wheat flour, salt, baking powder together twice. In a bowl beat egg whites. Add milk, oil, and honey. Blend. Add sifted dry ingredients and blend, but don't beat. Fold in beaten egg whites. Fry on pancake griddle until bubbly. Turn over and cook other side. Serve hot.

Put left-over pancakes in a plastic bag and freeze. When ready to serve again, pop in the toaster to reheat.

DRIED CORN CHIPS

½ cup dried corn*
½ cup boiling water

½ to 1 cup grated sharp cheddar
  cheese

Pour boiling water over dried corn. Let stand 5 minutes. Add 1 cup more water and let simmer 20-30 minutes, stirring occasionally to prevent sticking or scorching. When water is absorbed, pour corn in blender and puree. Add cheese and puree some more. Spread in a thin layer on well-buttered cookie sheet. Sprinkle lightly with seasoning salt of your choice. Bake in low oven (250°-275° F.) until partially dried. Score with a pizza cutter, so it will fall into uniform chips when completely dry. Bake until quite dry but not brown. It will dry more when cool. With spatula carefully lift chips off pan and cool on rack. Delicious plain or used for dip chips.

*Canned corn or "old" frozen corn can be used also.

87

FAUN'S CORN CHOWDER

1 cup dried corn
1½ cups boiling water
4 large potatoes, diced
2 tbsp butter
2 tbsp dried chopped onions
¼ cup dried peppers (optional)
1 cup chopped celery
2 cups water

1 tsp salt
⅛ tsp pepper
¼ tsp paprika
3 tbsp flour or cornstarch
2 cups whole milk
Dried parsley flakes
2 cups TVP bacon bits

Put corn in one bowl. In another bowl combine onions and peppers, snipped small with scissors. Pour 1 cup boiling water over corn and ½ cup boiling water over onion and peppers. Let stand 5 minutes. Simmer corn, stirring occasionally. Add more water if necessary to prevent scorching, while preparing other ingredients.

Melt butter and add drained reconstituted onion and peppers (reserving liquid). Cook until tender. (Peppers may remain quite leathery.) Add potatoes, water and seasonings. Simmer until potatoes are tender. Make paste of flour and ⅓ cup water. Add to potato mixture. Add milk and cook until slightly thickened, stirring constantly. Add cooked corn and heat through, but don't boil. Sprinkle TVP bacon bits with parsley flakes on top for serving. Makes 6 servings.

CORN BREAD

1 cup dried corn, coarsely ground
1 cup sifted flour
   (preferably whole wheat)
4 tsp baking powder
¾ tsp salt

¼ cup brown sugar
2 eggs, beaten
1 cup milk
¼ cup oil

Sift together twice cornmeal, flour, baking powder and salt into mixing bowl. Stir in brown sugar. Combine beaten egg, milk and oil. Add to dry ingredients and blend together with a spoon, not a beater. Pour into greased 9″ square pan and bake 25 minutes at 375°-400° F. Cut into squares and serve hot. This recipe can be used for corn muffins.

DRIED POTATO-CORN CASSEROLE

1 cup dried potato slices,
   crushed and pressed down
   in cup
½ cup dried corn
1½ cups boiling water
1 tbsp chopped dried onion

½ cup milk
3 eggs
½ tsp salt
1 cup cubed sharp cheddar
   cheese
2 tbsp butter

Drying Vegetables and Herbs

Mix onion, potatoes and corn in bowl. Pour boiling water over and let stand 5 minutes. Simmer 10-15 minutes. Cool slightly by dipping the cooking pan in cold water so hot mixture won't break the blender container. Pour mixture into blender and add all other ingredients. Cover. Blend at high speed until potatoes are grated. Pour into greased 1½-quart casserole or glass loaf pan. Bake 35-40 minutes at 350°-375° F. Serves 4-6.

BAKED CELERY

1 cup dried celery
¼ cup dried onion slices
½ cup dried mushrooms
¾ cup boiling water
½ can cream of celery soup

½ cup coarse bread crumbs
1 tbsp butter
¼ cup slivered almonds
Parmesan cheese

Pour boiling water over celery, onion rings and mushrooms. Let stand 5 minutes. Heat soup and combine with reconstituted vegetables. Bake 30 minutes at 325°-350° F. Brown crumbs and nuts in butter slightly. Sprinkle crumbs over baked food and return to oven for an additional 10 minutes. Sprinkle cheese on top just before serving. Makes 4 servings.

FANCY BAKED CELERY CASSEROLE

2 cups boiling water
2 cups dried celery pieces
  or 4 heaping cups sliced celery
½ cup boiling water
½ cup mushrooms or
1 can sliced mushrooms

1 can sliced water chestnuts,
  optional
1 can diced red pimentos, optional
½ cup dry bread crumbs
2 tbsp butter
½ cup sliced almonds
½ cup grated cheese, optional

Pour boiling water over celery and let stand five minutes. Cook until quite tender. Pour boiling water over mushrooms and let stand 5 minutes. Use remaining unabsorbed water in soup as it heats.

Combine celery, mushrooms, chestnuts and pimentos. Heat soup and pour over vegetables. Bake for 20 minutes at 325°-350° F. Slightly brown nuts and crumbs in butter, sprinkle on top and bake 10 minutes more. Makes 4-6 servings.

Sprinkle top with Parmesan cheese before serving. Or sprinkle grated cheese just before adding bread crumb-nuts mixture.

ESCALLOPED POTATOES

2 cups dried potatoes, packed   1 cup canned milk
2 cups boiling water

Pour boiling water over potatoes. Let stand 5 minutes. In greased 1-quart casserole pour potatoes. Pour canned milk over them. Bake at 325°-350° F. until potatoes are tender. Sprinkle with Parmesan cheese, if desired.

Generally, no salt is necessary.

SHIPWRECK STEW

½ cup sliced dried celery
¾ cup dried onion slices
2 cups boiling water
2 cups ground gluten
2 beef-flavored bouillon cubes
Oil for browning gluten,
  preferably olive oil
2 cups kidney beans

3 cups diced potatoes
¼ cup uncooked brown rice
1 tsp chili powder
1 tsp Worcestershire sauce
1 can tomato soup
about 12 slices dried tomato, whirled
  in blender
1 soup can of water

Pour 1 cup boiling water over celery and onions. Let stand five minutes. Brown gluten in large, heavy skillet which has a tight-fitting lid. Disslve bouillon in one cup of the boiling water and add to browned gluten. Let simmer a few minutes while preparing other ingredients. Heat tomato soup and add dry tomato powder in a separate pan, to which add chili powder and Worcestershire sauce. Add soup can of water and bring to a boil. Remove gluten from skillet.

In layers, place reconstituted onions and celery, potatoes, rice, gluten, beans. Pour tomato sauce over all. Simmer without removing lid for 60 minutes. With a fork test for tenderness of vegetables and rice. If necessary cook a few minutes longer. If using beef-flavored TVP instead of gluten, sprinkle on top during last 15-20 minutes of cooking. Makes about 6 servings. Sprinkle with Parmesan cheese, if desired.

Note: This stew can be cooked in a crockpot, at least 8 hours.

UNTIDY JOSEPHS (SLOPPY JOES)

2 cups ground gluten flavored
  with 2 bouillon cubes
  dissolved in a little hot
  water
6 slices dried tomatoes
1 tbsp dried chopped onion
½ cup boiling water

1 tbsp flour
2 tbsp ketchup
2 tsp Worcestershire sauce
1 bay leaf
½ tsp chili powder
½ cup water

90

Drying Vegetables and Herbs

Whirl tomatoes in blender until powdered. Combine onion and tomato powder with boiling water and simmer in small saucepan while browning the gluten in a little oil in a frying pan. Add dissolved bouillon and simmer a few minutes to allow gluten to absorb flavor. Add flour to browned gluten. Mix well, then add all other ingredients, including the tomato sauce. Simmer 20-30 minutes, stirring occasionally to prevent sticking. Serve on buns. Makes 6 servings.

MUSHROOM SOUP

1 cup dried mushrooms
2 quarts boiling water
1 medium onion, chopped, *or*
   ¼ cup dried chopped onion
¼ cup butter or margarine
4 medium potatoes, pared and cut
   in rather large chunks

2 bouillon cubes,
   softened in a little water
Salt to taste
Dairy sour cream (optional)
Parmesan cheese (optional)
TVP bacon bits (optional)

Pour boiling water over mushrooms and let stand 5 minutes. Simmer until tender. Drain, saving water. Lightly brown mushrooms and onions in 3 tbsp of the butter in a heavy 4-quart pan. Stir in remaining water, potatoes, and bouillon cubes. Heat to boiling. Reduce heat. Simmer 35-40 minutes. Stir in remaining butter. Season. Serve with dollops of sour cream, if desired. Or sprinkle with Parmesan cheese. Or sprinkle with bacon bits. makes about six 1-cup servings.

CREAM OF ONION SOUP

1 cup dried onion slices
1 cup boiling water
Dash ground mace
¼ cup flour
1 quart milk
2 chicken-style bouillon cubes,
   softened in a little boiling water

1 egg yolk, beaten
Salt to taste
Dried parsley flakes (or
   fresh snipped)
Grated Parmesan cheese

Pour boiling water over onion slices and let stand 5 minutes. Lift slices out of water (reserve liquid) and cook in butter in large saucepan until golden brown. Sprinkle with mace. Stir in flour. Cook over low heat, stirring constantly until smooth and bubbly. Stir in cold milk. Cook over low heat, stirring occasionally, until slightly thickened. Stir in bouillon cube mixture and onion liquid. Cook 5 minutes. Remove from heat. Stir small amount of soup into beaten egg yolk. Return mixture to soup. Heat until hot, but do not boil. Season with salt. Serve with parsley flakes and Parmesan cheese sprinkled over top. Makes 6 to 8 servings.

TOMATO SAUCE

In blender, powder dried tomato slices. Put in saucepan and combine with boiling water. Simmer. Season as desired with seasoning salts, chili powder. Twelve slices will make about 1½ cups of tomato sauce.

If a blender is not available, pour boiling water to cover dried tomato slices. Let stand 5 minutes, then simmer. Push through a strainer and add seasonings.

MUSHROOM-GLUTEN BALLS

2 cups ground gluten
½ tsp salt
1 large egg
1 tbsp dried milk
1 tbsp dried chopped onion
1 tsp onion soup powder

1 cup dried sliced mushrooms
1 cup boiling water
3 green peppers, finely chopped,
 or equivalent dried
1 large onion finely chopped
 or equivalent dried
½ tsp chopped parsley

Pour boiling water over mushrooms (and peppers and onion, if using dried products) and let stand 5 minutes. Simmer vegetables until tender. Combine gluten, salt, egg, dried milk, chopped onion, onion soup mix and form into small balls. Brown in oil. Combine with vegetables and season to taste. Serve piping hot over cooked rice, scrambled eggs or Chinese noodles.

ZUCCHINI CASSEROLE

2 cups dried sliced or grated
 zucchini*
1½ cups boiling water
1 tbsp dried onion
1-2 slices stale bread, broken in
 pieces (toasting makes it better).
 Use enough bread to absorb
 moisture of zucchini mixture.

Salt to taste
2 eggs, beaten
1 cup grated cheese

Pour boiling water over zucchini and onion and let stand 5 minutes. Simmer until mushy. Add bread and stir until absorbed. Add beaten eggs. Pour into greased casserole. Top with cheese. Bake at 300°-325° F. 20-30 minutes.

*This recipe can be made from dried or fresh zucchini and large, thick-skinned zucchini can be peeled and used.

ZUCCHINI BREAD

2 cups dried zucchini
1½ cups boiling water
3 cups unsifted flour
1 tsp salt
1 tsp cinnamon
1 tsp baking soda

1¼ tsp baking powder
3 eggs, beaten
2 cups brown sugar
1 cup oil
1 tsp vanilla
1 cup chopped nuts

Pour boiling water over zucchini and let stand 5 minutes. Sift dry ingredients together twice. Whirl zucchini in blender. Beat eggs. Add brown sugar, oil, vanilla and beat well. Add zucchini with sifted dry ingredients. Fold in chopped nuts and pour into two greased and floured loaf pans. Bake 50-60 minutes at 325°-350° F.

PREPARING AND DRYING VEGETABLES

(These are *suggested guidelines* only, because of variables in climate and food.)

Vegetable	How to Prepare	Steaming Time (Minutes)	Dryness Test	Use
Asparagus (Tender tips only)	Wash thoroughly. Cut tips in half.	4 to 5	Leathery to brittle	Use as fresh.
Beans, Green (Mature but tender)	Wash thoroughly. Cut in pieces or lengthwise.	10 to 20	Brittle	Use as fresh or in recipes.
Beets	Cook as usual. Cool, peel. Quarter or slice ¼" or in shoestrings.	None	Tough, & leathery	Use a *little* water in re-constituting because of bleeding.
Broccoli	Trim & cut as for serving. Wash thoroughly. Quarter stalks lengthwise.	3 to 3½	Brittle	Use as fresh or in recipes.
Brussels Sprouts	Cut in half, lengthwise through stem.	6 to 7	Brittle	Use as fresh.
Cabbage	Remove outer leaves, quarter and core. Cut into ⅛" strips.	2½ to 3 wilted	Tough to brittle	Use as fresh in salads and recipes.
Carrots (Crisp, tender)	Wash thoroughly. Cut off roots & tops. New carrots can be scrubbed, but peel older ones. Grate or cut in ⅛"-¼" strips or rounds.	3 to 5	Tough, leathery	Use as fresh or in recipes.

Vegetable	How to Prepare	Steaming Time (Minutes)	Dryness Test	Use
Cauliflower	Prepare as for serving.	4 to 5	Tough to brittle	Reconstituted raw, or simmered.
Celery (Good for table)	Trim & wash. Slice stalks ¼". If celery is to be powdered, do not steam. Use leaves.	2 to 3	Brittle	Use in recipes.
Corn	Husk, trim. Steam until milk is set. Cut off cob.	10 to 15 (on cob)	Dry, brittle	Simmer and use as fresh. In recipes. Ground for cornmeal.
Eggplant	Wash, trim, slice ¼".	3 to 4	Brittle	Use in recipes.
Cucumber (Table condition)	Peel and slice ¼".	4 to 6	Brittle	Use for flavoring & in salads.
Mushrooms (Use only edible varieties!)	Wash & sort. Remove stems. Use stems for powder. Use whole or slice.	None	Dry & leathery	Use in usual mushroom recipes.
Garlic (Powdered or clove)	Remove husks, separate cloves. Slice or leave whole.	None	Brittle	Seasoning.
Herbs (Mature, no wilted leaves)	Wash & sort. Shake off water. Use whole.	None	Brittle	Low drying temperature, about 110° F.
Greens (Beets, Chard, Spinach, etc.)	Trim & wash gently but thoroughly. Cut out stems if necessary.	2 to 4 only	Brittle	Use as fresh.

Vegetable	How to Prepare	Steaming Time (Minutes)	Dryness Test	Use
Okra	Wash, trim & slice crosswise 1/4".	4 to 5	Brittle or tough	Use in recipes.
Onions	Wash & remove outer "paper." Remove crown & tops. Slice 1/8-1/4" or cube or chop.	None	Brittle	Use in recipes. Seasoning.
Onion Powder	Same as above.	None	Brittle	Powder for seasoning salt.
Peas (Tender, full grown)	Shell. Do not wash. Grade for size & maturity.	5 to 15	Brittle	Work quickly to retain quality and flavor.
Pea pods	Wash & strip lengthwise, "string."	2 to 4	Brittle	Use as dip chips.
Peppers (Red & green)	Sort & wash. Core & slice 1/4" strips or snip small.	3 to 6 or None	Brittle	Use in recipes & soups.
Potatoes (white)	Wash & peel. Slice 1/8", cube or shoestring 1/4" strips, or grate.	6 to 10 translucent	Brittle	Use in recipes or as dip chips. Grated for hash browns.
Potatoes (sweet)	Precook as for table use. Peel & trim. Slice 1/4".	No further pretreatment	Leathery	Use in recipes.
Squash—Pumpkin, Banana, Hubbard	Wash, de-seed, peel, slice 1/8" or 1/4".	2½ to 3	Tough to brittle	See Vegetable Suggestions.
Summer	Wash, trim, cut 1/4".	2½ to 3	Tough to brittle	Reconstitute, season & serve.

Vegetable	How to Prepare	Steaming Time (Minutes)	Dryness Test	Use
Tomatoes (for stewing)	Scald, chill, peel, slice or quarter. Cut pear, plum or cherry tomatoes in half.	None or 3	Leathery to brittle	See Vegetable Suggestions. Will scorch easily. Over-ripe spots may go black.
Turnips & Rutabagas	Peel, trim, slice, dice or shoestring.	8 to 10	Leathery	Handle carefully to avoid sticking.
Zucchini	Wash, trim, cut ⅛"-¼", or grate, according to expected use.	1 to 3	Tough to brittle	See Vegetable Suggestions.

Chapter 9

MAKE YOUR OWN PREPARED CEREAL

The prices stamped on the boxes of the huge array of prepared cereals on the supermarket shelves is enough to discourage an economizing homemaker. But the promotion campaigns have convinced her children that prepared cold cereal is the only acceptable breakfast.

How can you beat it? Make your own, of course, and you'll be serving your family a much more nutritious breakfast than you can ever get out of a box. FDA tests have found most of the commercial products deficient in food value.

Homemade granola is not only a delicious breakfast food, but a desirable snack as well. It can also be used in recipes for added nutrition. Use my recipe given below and try some of the following ideas. (As you become accustomed to its use, you'll think of many more.)

Serve as cold cereal. Snip dried fruits of your choice and sprinkle over the top. Serve with milk or cream for a real day-starter.

Add a cup or two to your favorite bread recipe.

Sprinkle over ice cream for a crunchy, chewy topping.

Crush in the blender and use for graham cracker pie crust.

Sauté in a little butter and sprinkle over any vegetable.

Add to your favorite pancake recipe.

Sprinkle over cooked or instant puddings.

Use as a filler for cinnamon rolls.

Use as a substitute for part of the flour in muffins or cookies.

Top casseroles.

Top coffee cake.

99

Recipes

WHEAT FLAKES

½ cup whole wheat flour   ¼ to ½ tsp salt
2 cups boiling water

Mix with a good egg beater flour, salt and water in a double boiler. Be sure all lumps are beaten out. Cook about 20 minutes or until thick. Adjust amount of water to suit yourself, to make it the consistency of puree for leather. Flavor with brown sugar to taste. Add nutmeg or cinnamon or vanilla, if desired. Follow directions for making fruit leather. Dry in oven or dehydrator until completely dry. It should break into pieces when taken off the plastic wrap and can be used for cereal with milk. Or you may prefer not drying it so hard and eating it for snacks, like leather.

GRANOLA

4 cups old-fashioned oatmeal   1 cup sunflower seeds, *or*
4 cups rolled wheat or wheat   1 cup pumpkin seeds, optional
  flakes   ½ cup water
1 to 1½ cups coconut   ½ cup oil
1 cup wheat germ   ¾ cup honey
1 cup sesame seeds   1 tsp salt
½ cup powdered whey

Mix together dry ingredients in large bowl. Mix together water, oil and honey in small saucepan. Warm but do not boil. Pour honey mixture over dry ingredients. Mix well. Spread on 2 large cookie sheets and bake at 225°-250° F. for 2 hours, stirring occasionally.

Or Granola can be dried in the dehydrator in 5 to 6 hours at about 140° F., and you'll think you have two different recipes.

The advantage of "cooking" granola in the dehydrator is that vitamins are not destroyed, as with the higher heat.

100

Chapter 10
MISCELLANEOUS SAVERS

If you live in a humid climate, crackers lose their crispness. Recrisp them in the oven or dehydrator.

Recipes

CROUTONS

If you have bread that is not too fresh, stack two or three slices together and cut off crusts. Cube the slices of bread. If bread is still quite soft, let it dry more before cutting so the pieces will not be squashed together. Use a sharp knife so pieces can be cut in uniform cubes. The cubes can be dehydrated plain or can be seasoned with seasoning salt, spices, or Parmesan cheese. Combine seasonings in a paper sack and drop cubes in. Shake so cubes are uniformly coated. Spread plastic wrap over the dryer shelf or oven rack and lay the cubes on it. This keeps crumbs from dropping through. Croutons will dry in two or three hours, or less, depending on how dry the bread is at the beginning of the process.

Use croutons sprinkled over salads or soups, just before serving so they don't become soggy.

Price packaged croutons and compute your savings!

SESAME CRISPS

Your favorite bread recipe   ½ to 1 cup sesame seeds
Reserve 1 loaf portion when baking

Work seeds into dough. Divide into portions and bake in small frozen juice *metal* cans. (Do not use foil-covered cardboard cans.) Let rise almost double in bulk. Bake in preheated oven at 350°-375° F., for 30-40 minutes. Cool thoroughly. Slice thin. Arrange on drying racks. Takes about 3 to 4 hours to dry. Store in cans or waxed paper. Better if consumed within 2 or 3 weeks. If desired, sprinkle *very lightly* with seasoning salt before drying.

SESAME THINS

1 cup whole wheat flour
6 tbsp oil
½ cup water

½ tsp sea salt
Sesame seeds

Emulsify oil and water and add dry ingredients. Knead for 5 minutes and let rest 10 minutes. Divide into 2 parts and roll out each part on an oiled cookie sheet. Salt and sprinkle with sesame seeds and roll again. Mark in squares and prick with a fork. Bake at 350° F. about 10 minutes.

Or for dryer, dry until very crisp. Use different seasoned salts as preferred. Score with a pizza cutter before drying.

CRACKERS

3 cups quick oats, uncooked
2 cups whole wheat flour
1 cup wheat germ
1 cup water

3 tbsp honey
½ tsp salt
¾ cup oil

Mix and roll on two large cookie sheets clear to the edge or turn sheets over and use pan without edges. These must be rolled thin. Sprinkle with sea salt. Cut into desired shape; bake at 325° F. for 30 minutes. They must be dry and crisp. Instead of sea salt, use savory salt, vege-sal, or other seasoning salts, as desired.

For dryer, roll very thin and place on sheets of foil or plastic wrap. Dry until very crisp.

SAVORY DRESSING

3 tbsp butter
1 medium onion, chopped, *or*
  2 tbsp reconstituted dried onion
½ cup diced celery, *or*
  2 tbsp dried celery,
  reconstituted

2 cups whole wheat bread crumbs
½ tsp salt
½ tsp sage, *or*
  sprig of dried sage, crumbled

Melt butter in a skillet and slightly cook onion and celery in it. Add bread crumbs, salt and sage. Mix together well. Add about ½ cup water, or enough that mixture is dampened but not soaked.

One cup brown rice can be substituted for 1 cup of bread crumbs.

One-half cup pinenuts or sunflower seeds and sesame seeds can be added for variation and extra flavor.

Note: If bread is not dry, put it in the dehydrator for an hour or two, or leave out overnight to dry. If soft bread is used for dressing, you'll probably have soggy dressing. I get best results by using dry bread crumbs which I keep in the freezer. I grind quite a bit at once, then have them ready for any recipe calling for bread crumbs.

EGG NOODLES

2 cups flour   2 or 3 eggs
1 tsp salt   Water

Mix ingredients together, gradually adding just enough water to make a very stiff dough. Roll out thin into an oblong on canvas-covered board. Flour board and rolling pin heavily. When thin enough, flour top of dough. Roll as for a jelly roll. Cut roll into three shorter ones and stack for quicker cutting. With fingers, lift high and gently tumble the noodles and let unroll as much as possible. Arrange on dryer or oven rack. It doesn't take long to dry them to brittle stage.

YOGURT

You can make yogurt in your dehydrator only if you can keep the temperature between 120°-105° F. Test it with an oven thermometer. It takes about 5 hours. If temperature is too hot (over 120° F.) the yogurt bacteria will die. If temperature drops below 100° F. plain old sour milk bacteria will develop.

4 cups whole milk   1 heaping tbsp unflavored yogurt*
½ cup instant powdered milk

Combine powdered milk with whole milk and heat to boiling point for a few seconds only. Cool to 120° F. Remove ¼ cup of boiled and cooled milk and mix in yogurt. Stir to make a thin consistency. Return this "thickening" to the boiled milk and stir well. Pour into clean glass jars. Screw on new lids and place in the middle of the dehydrator. Do not stir while setting. The more you stir, the thinner it becomes. At the end of 5 hours, check to see if it is set. If so, remove from dehydrator and cool immediately. If not set, check every few minutes until it sets up. If yogurt bubbles and starts to separate, it has been in the dehydrator too long.

Dried fruit of your choice for flavoring can be added just before cooling. It need not be reconstituted because it will draw the necessary moisture from the yogurt and makes a tasty, thick product. Fold fruit in gently to prevent thinning.

*Unflavored commercial yogurt can be purchased at the health food store. Use this or a start from your last batch. Yogurt will keep in the refrigerator for about 1 week. If yogurt is made once a week, a fresh starter is always available.

TVP (Textured Vegetable Protein)

Of course TVP can be purchased commercially, flavored or unflavored. To make your own, simply soak soybeans for a couple of hours or overnight, whichever fits your time schedule. Cook until tender. The water may be almost completely absorbed. If not, drain. Grind in food grinder on medium or fine disc. Dehydrate in dryer.

Green "cooking" soybeans cook faster than tan "sprouting" soybeans.

For a stick-to-the-ribs, chewy beakfast or lunch, try adding homemade granules to canned or reconstituted cooked dried fruit. Let the granules soften in the juice. Add sesame seeds and/or sunflower seeds and top with yogurt.

When using TVP as a meat substitute, meat flavoring—such as bouillon cubes—can be dissolved in hot water and added as part of the soaking water (in the initial preparation) to impart a beef or chicken flavor. Check your health food store for flavorings.

Below are some precautions and helps to use TVP in recipes more effectively.

To reconstitute unflavored granules use:

1 cup dry granules	1 cup hot water
1 tsp instant bouillon	½ tsp salt, more or less, to suit your taste

Let stand 15 minutes. It will be ready for use in any recipe. Yield should be at least two cups reconstituted, or the equivalent of one pound ground beef.

Two bouillon cubes equal one teaspoon instant bouillon.

To reconstitute commercial flavored granules use:

1 cup dry granules	Salt to taste
1 cup hot water	

When substituting soy granules for meat in a recipe, remember that soy granules are already cooked, so should not be cooked in the preparation as long as meat.

If using dried onions, reconstitute at the same time and in the same water with the granules.

If using soy granules to substitute for meat in a casserole (in patties or balls) sauté the onion in a little oil until tender. Then add the reconstituted granules and seasonings and simmer for a few minutes.

104

Miscellaneous Savers

If using in sauce (such as spaghetti) add the granules last to the sauce and let stand a while without cooking to absorb flavors of the sauce. Then reheat just before serving.

When frying granules for use in a recipe, always use a little oil in the pan to prevent sticking. Olive oil gives a meat-like flavor.

"MEATBALLS" OR PATTIES FROM TVP

2 cups reconstituted granules
  (1 cup dry)
1 large egg
1 tbsp dry milk
1 tbsp dried minced onion (or
  1 small fresh onion chopped)

1 tbsp flour
salt to taste
¼ tsp brown sugar (optional)

Mix all ingredients well. Form into patties or balls and brown in oil.

Gluten*

Gluten can be made by hand or in an electric dough-mixer. When making by hand, use the basic amounts given below and knead thoroughly a good 10 minutes, pounding and rolling dough also to develop the gluten completely. Then follow all the other instructions outlined below after the words "take out the dough hook."

Electric dough mixer method:
9 cups cold water in mixer bowl
18 cups fine whole wheat stoneground flour

To the water in mixer bowl add 6 cups flour, beating until well blended. Then add another 6 cups. The last 6 cups must be sprinkled in slowly because of stiffness. Moisture content will vary with different wheat. Be careful that dough doesn't clean the bowl as in breadmaking. If it gets to that point, add a little water to restore moisture. Knead 5-10 minutes. Remove bowl from its base and take out dough hook.

---

*Vernice G. Rosenvall, Mabel H. Miller and Dora D. Flack, *Wheat for Man . . . Why and How* (Bookcraft: Salt Lake City, Utah, rev. 1975) pp. 51-52.

Add 2 inches of water on top of dough. With hands, clean it away from sides and bottom of bowl. Let stand about an hour. Pour first starch water off into another pan. Save all water from gluten-making because it contains vitamins and minerals. Use it for breadmaking, mixing dry milk, gravies, soups, sauces, eggnog, banana drink, frozen fruit ices, etc.

Set colander containing many small holes in pan of water. Add about 2 cups dough at a time to colander. In pan, squeeze fingers into dough and pull it away from holes. It will seem to come apart and you think you'll lose it. Then suddenly it will act like bubble gum. Pick it up with both hands and, in a second pan, squeeze it under the cleaner water until the sandy feeling is gone (water should run clear). Set it aside and let rest in colander at least a half-hour to drain off as much moisture as possible. This makes about two pounds of raw gluten.

Raw gluten can be prepared as a substitute for meat in a variety of ways and can be prepared and refrigerated or frozen for future use, discussed in detail in *Wheat for Man* and in *The Gluten Book*, by LeArta Moulton, published and distributed by The Gluten Co., Inc., P.O. Box 482, Provo, Utah 84601.

Only the method for doing "ground beef" will be discussed here, relating to the recipes included in this book. When gluten is to be used for patties, meatballs, casseroles, etc. instead of ground beef, place raw gluten on lightly oiled cookie sheet or 2-3 bread pans. Push from the center out and stretch until it is fairly even, ½-inch thick. Bake 15 minutes in preheated oven at 325°-350° F. Twist fork in bubbles and thick-raised areas to let out steam. Cook another 15 minutes, or until it springs back when pressed.

Remove from oven and, if gluten seems crisp on top or bottom, either put it in a plastic bag, or fold the large sheet of gluten until the steam adjusts the texture evenly, or sprinkle water on it. When there are no crisp areas, run it through the meat grinder on medium disc, or grate on largest holes of a shredder. It will be soft and pliable. Refrigerate or freeze for future use in hamburger, sauces, patties, sausages, casseroles or desserts.

To make hamburgers, place ground gluten in a bowl. Season with dried onion soup powder. Stir in egg and chopped or dried onion. (Dried onion soup mix may be used.) A little instant bouillon, dissolved, can be added for flavoring also, if desired. Brown in oil in a skillet. Cover and slowly steam 5 minutes to bring out flavor.

Gluten Jerky

(Courtesy of Ruth Laughlin)

Make gluten according to preceding recipe. (To make one pound of raw gluten, use 4½ cups water and 8-9 cups whole wheat flour.)

Spread the ball of drained gluten on a cookie sheet about ½" to ¾" thick. Partially freeze for easy cutting into thin strips about 1/8" thick.

In a shallow roaster or broiler pan, place the broth (recipe below) and bring to a boil. Drop gluten strips into boiling broth. Boil hard until most of broth is absorbed. Add 3 tbsp. liquid smoke (the equivalent in other seasonings of your preference, such as onion, garlic, and/or celery salt, soy sauce, Worcestershire sauce). Continue simmering on low heat until remaining broth is absorbed.

If drying jerky in oven, cover cookie sheet with plastic wrap. Straighten strips on plastic and dry with oven door ajar.

If using a dehydrator, spread plastic wrap over shelf or use three thicknesses of net to catch possible drips. Turn dehydrator up to about 150°. You may wish to turn it down in an hour to finish drying to a tough leathery consistency.

BROTH

4 cups water
2 heaping tbsp beef flavored base
1 tbsp ham flavoring

1 tbsp bacon bits
1 tbsp Kitchen Bouquet

Pumpkin or Squash Flour

In the autumn and especially at Halloween, pumpkin and squash is plentiful and inexpensive. As I drive by the fruit/vegetable stands, it hurts me to know that most of it will be wasted. Don't let it waste. Dry according to instructions on the preceding chart for vegetables. Pumpkin peel will come off easier if steamed. Decide which works best for you. Thick-skinned squash is so difficult to peel that you may feel it is not worth the trouble. Dry to the brittle stage, and pumpkin and squash can be used interchangeably in recipes. Experiment with your own regular pumpkin recipes.

Dried squash or pumpkin can be simmered and blended to the consistency of canned pumpkin and can be substituted for canned pumpkin.

Brittle squash or pumpkin can be powdered almost completely in the blender. With a sieve, separate the powder from the bits and store in separate containers in the refrigerator for specific uses, as follows:

Pumpkin powder can be used as part of the flour in muffins, pancakes, waffles. Use ¼ cup pumpkin powder and ¾ cup flour for each cup of flour required in a recipe. This gives the resulting product a lively color, plus moistness.

Pumpkin bits left in the sieve can be reconstituted and simmered and used like canned pumpkin in pie or pumpkin bread or cookies.

PUMPKIN MUFFINS

1½ cups sifted whole wheat flour
½ cup pumpkin flour
½ tsp salt
3 tsp baking powder
2 eggs, beaten

1 cup milk
4 tbsp brown sugar *or*
3 tbsp honey
4 tbsp oil

Sift together dry ingredients. Combine beaten eggs, milk, honey, oil in mixing bowl. Stir in dry ingredients only until blended, but not smooth. Bake in greased muffin tins 20-30 minutes at 375°-400° F. Makes 1 dozen. Variations:
—Add ½ cup chopped nuts.
—Add ½ cup chopped dates.
—Mix 3 tbsp sugar with 1 tsp cinnamon and sprinkle on top.

PUMPKIN BREAD

½ cup dried pumpkin bits
½ cup boiling water
1½ cups sifted whole wheat flour
1 tsp soda
½ tsp salt
½ tsp nutmeg

½ tsp cinnamon
1¼ cups brown sugar
2 eggs, beaten
½ cup oil
⅓ cup water
½ cup nuts

Let pumpkin simmer 15-20 minutes. Return to blender and add more water as necessary as it whirls until you achieve the consistency of canned pumpkin. Sift dry ingredients together twice. Combine beaten eggs, pumpkin, oil and water in mixing bowl. Add dry ingredients and mix well. Add nuts. Bake in 2 small loaf pans 7½" × 3½" or 1 large pan 8½" × 4½" 45-60 minutes at 325°-350° F.

Miscellaneous Savers

PUMPKIN CHIFFON PIE

(Makes 1 deep 10" pie or 2 small pies)

1½ cups dried pumpkin or squash
Boiling water to cover
½ cup brown sugar
2 egg yolks (large)
1½ cups milk
½ tsp salt

½ tsp cinnamon
½ tsp nutmeg
1 tbsp unflavored gelatin
¼ cup cold water
2 egg whites
½ cup brown sugar

Place dried pumpkin in a bowl and cover with boiling water. Let stand 5 minutes. Then simmer until tender in 2-quart pan. Puree in blender until smooth. Add more water if needed so blender is not overworked and return to pan.

Beat egg yolks and brown sugar. Add milk. Pour egg-milk mixture into blender and whirl to clean out pumpkin residue. Add to pumpkin in pan and cook on medium heat 10-15 minutes, stirring occasionally to prevent scorching. Dissolve gelatin in water in bowl. Let stand. Add small amount of cooked pumpkin mixture to gelatin. Add salt and spices. Stir until smooth and add to cooked mixture. Beat egg whites, adding sugar gradually. Beat hard 3 or 4 minutes to dissolve sugar. Fold into cooked mixture and pour into baked pie shell. Chill.

Top with whipped cream just before serving. For a delicious topping variation, lightly toast coconut in oven. Sprinkle on top.

BIBLIOGRAPHY

Articles

Caesar, Liz, "Leather You Can Eat," *Riverside Press-Enterprise,* Riverside, California, July 27, 1975.

Flack, Dora D., "Fruit Leather," *Organic Gardening,* August, 1972.

_____, "Let's Make Dried Fruit Leather," *Ensign,* June 1972.

Rosenkranz, Patrick, "Sun-Drying Fruit in Oregon," *Organic Gardening and Farming,* September 1975.

Rothert, Yvonne, "Canby Homemaker Puts by Harvest," *The Oregonian,* August 20, 1975.

Pamphlets

Bardwell, Flora H., and Salunkhe, D. K., *Home Drying of Fruits and Vegetables,* Utah State University Extension Service, Logan, Utah.

Boie, Shirley A., *Herb Teas for Health,* Boie Enterprises, Los Angeles, California.

Nutritive Value of Foods, Home and Garden Bulletin No. 72, Washington, D.C., United States Government Printing Office, 1971.

Books

Anderson, M. L. and Andrews, J. M., *Nature's Way,* Crabtree, Oregon: JMA Productions, 1974.

Bills, Jay and Shirley, *Home Food Dehydrating,* Bountiful, Utah: Horizon Publishers, 1974.

Densley, Barbara, *The ABC's of Home Food Dehydration,* Bountiful, Utah: Horizon Publishers, 1973.

Dickey, Esther, *Passport to Survival,* Salt Lake City, Utah: Bookcraft, 1969.

Farm Journal Food Editors, *How to Dry Fruits and Vegetables at Home,* Philadelphia, Pennsylvania: The Countryside Press, 1975.

Flack, Dora D., *Fun with Fruit Preservation,* Bountiful, Utah: Horizon Publishers, 1973.

MacManiman, Gen, *Dry It—You'll Like It,* Seattle, Washington: Evergreen Printing Co., 1974.

Salsbury, Barbara G., *Just Add Water,* Bountiful, Utah: Horizon Publishers, 1972.

_____. *Tasty Imitations,* Bountiful, Utah: Horizon Publishers, 1973.

_____. *Just in Case,* Salt Lake City, Utah: Bookcraft, Inc., 1975.

Wheeler, emme, *Home Food Dehydration,* Seattle, Washington: Craftsman and Met Press, 1974.

INDEX TO CHARTS AND RECIPES

Charts

Fruit preparing and drying, 72-77
Vegetable preparing and drying, 94-97

Leather and Related Goodies

Aplets, 46
Apple and variations, 41
Applesauce, 41
Apricot and variations, 42
Banana, 42
Blackberry, 42
Blueberry, 42
Cherry and variations, 42
Cotlets, 46
Cranberry-Date, 43
Fruitlets, 46
Grape, 43
Grapefruit, 43
Lemon, 43
Limon, 43
Mulberry, 42
Nectarine, 43
Peach, 44
Peach-Pineapple, 44
Pear, 44
Pearlets, 46
Persimmon, 45
Pineapple, 44
Pineapple-Strawberry-Rhubarb, 44
Pinwheels, Light-Colored Filling, 47
  Dark-Colored Filling, 47
Plum, 44
Plum-Apricot, 45
Plum Pearlets, 46
Raspberry, 45
Rhubarb, 45
Strawblets, 46
Tomato, 47

Fruits

Apricot-Coconut Cookies, 66
Apricot Snowballs, 66
Banana Coconut Bars, 67
Banana Cookies, 67
Banana Nut Loaf, 67
Basic Stewed Fruit Mix, 52

Capped Fruit-filled Cookies, 55
Carobcote, 61
Chewy Apple Cookies, 64
Dried Apple Bread, 63
Dried Apple Cake or Pudding, 64
Dried Apple Turnovers, 65
Dried Apricot Bread, 66
Dried Apricot Cookies, 71
Dried Fruit Candies, 61
Dried Fruit Crisp, 56
Dried Fruit-filled Cookies, 54
Dried Fruit Tarts, 56
Dried Rhubarb Bread, 69
Dried Rhubarb Pie, 70
Favorite Fruit Cake, 59
Flavor-added Rice, 52
French Apple Pie, 65
Fruit Breakfast Drink, 56
Fruit Cake (old bottled fruit), 59
Fruit Candy, 62
Fruit Cobbler, 53
Fruit-filled Bars, 55
Fruit Muffins, 56
Fruit Oatmeal, 53
German Fruit Bread, 57
Golden Fruit Cup, 58
Gorp, 62
Granola Candy, 60
Hikers Honey Squares, 63
Old-Fashioned Plum Pudding, 68
Orange Dried-Pear Bars, 68
Peanut Butter Balls, 62
Pick-me-up Patties, 60
Plum Puffs, 68
Rhubarb Slush, 69
Rhubarb-Strawberry Dessert or Salad,
  70
Spring Shortcake, 70
Stewed Dried-Apple Combo, 58
Survival or Breakfast Bar, 60
Sweet Treats, 62
"Weight-Watcher" Apples, 63

Vegetables

Baked Celery, 89
Carrot Cake, 86
Carrot Salad, 85
Coleslaw, 84

Corn Bread, 88
Corn Pancakes, 87
Cream Cheese Icing, 86
Cream of Onion Soup, 91
Dried Bean-Burger Casserole, 85
Dried Cabbage Casserole, 84
Dried Corn, 86
Dried Corn Chips, 87
Dried Grated Carrot Cookies, 86
Dried Potato-Corn Casserole, 88
Dried String Beans, 85
Escalloped Potatoes, 90
Fancy Baked Celery Casserole, 89
Fast Hash, 85
Faun's Corn Chowder, 88
Burger Soup, 83
Mushroom-Gluten Balls 92
Shipwreck Stew, 90
Tomato Sauce, 92
Untidy Josephs (Sloppy Joes), 90
White Sauce, 84
Zucchini Bread, 93
Zucchini Casserole, 92

Prepared Cereal

Granola, 100
Wheat Flakes, 100

Miscellaneous Savers

Crackers, 102
Croutons, 101
Egg Noodles, 103
Gluten, 105
Gluten Jerky, 107
"Meatballs" or Patties from TVP, 105
Pumpkin or Squash Flour, 107
Pumpkin Muffins, 108
Pumpkin Bread, 108
Pumpkin Chiffon Pie, 109
Savory Dressing, 102
Sesame Crisps, 101
Sesame Thins, 102
TVP, 104
Yogurt, 103

SUBJECT INDEX

-A-

Apples, drying of, 50, 72
  uses of, 50
  for fruit leather, 41
Apricots, drying of, 50, 72
  uses of, 50
  for fruit leather, 42
Ascorbic acid, as pretreatment, 23
Asparagus, drying of, 94
Avocado, drying of, 50, 73
  uses of, 50

-B-

Bananas, drying of, 50
  uses of, 50
Beans, green, drying of, 94
  in recipes, 84
Beets, drying of, 94
  with mandarin oranges, 82
Berries, drying of, 50, 73
Blackberries, drying of, 73
Blanching, as pretreatment, 27
Blueberries, drying of, 73
Broccoli, drying of, 94
Brussels sprouts, drying of, 94

-C-

Cabbage, drying of, 94
  in recipes, 84, 85
Cantaloupe, drying of, 74
  uses of, 51
Car or camper drying, 15
Carrots, drying of, 94
  uses of, 82
  in recipes, 85, 86
Case hardening, 8
Cauliflower, drying of, 95
Celery, drying of, 95
  in recipes, 88, 89
Cherries, drying of, 74
  uses of, 51
  for fruit leather, 42
Citrus fruit, drying of, 74
Commercially dried food, 9
  dehydrated, 9

freeze-dried, 9
low-moisture dried, 9
Corn, drying of, 95
  in recipes, 86-88
Cranberries, drying of, 73
  uses of, 50
Cucumbers, drying of, 95

-D-

Dates, drying of, 75
Date sugar, making of, 51
Dehydrator
  airflow, 20
  construction points, 19-21
  drying capacity, 19
  economy, 19
  shelving, 20, 16
Dewberries, drying of, 74
Drying of food, ancient method, 1-2
  economical facets, 3-5
  less storage space required, 2
Drying rack, construction of, 11
  sketch of, 13
Dryness test
  See Preparation Charts, fruits, 72-77
  See Preparation Charts, vegetables, 94-97

-E-

Economy of dried foods, 2-5
  convenience foods, 3-5
  energy saved, 3
  no sugar required, 2
  small amounts, 2
  surplus produce, 2
Eggplant, drying of, 95
Enzymes, spoilage caused by, 6-8, 79
Equalizing moisture, in dried foods, 29

-F-

Figs, drying of, 75
Fruit mix, homemade, 51
  drying of, 75
Fruitlets, recipes for, 46

Subject Index

-G-

Garlic, drying of, 95
"Gilding the lily," 28
Glazed fruit, made from old fruit, 39
Gluten, making and using, 83, 106
Golden raisins, making of, 51
Gooseberries, drying of, 73
Granola, uses of, 101
Grapes, seedless (green), drying of, 75
  black ribber, 75
  tokay, 75
  uses of, 51
Greens, drying of, 95
  careful handling, 82
Guava, drying of, 76
  uses of, 51

-H-

Herbs, characteristics of growing, 80
  dried, care of, 80
  drying of, 80-81, 95
  mixed for seasonings, 80-81
  uses of, 80
Honey, when substituting for sugar, 52
Honey Dew, drying of, 74
Honey and lemon juice, as pretreatment, 26
Huckleberries, drying of, 73
Hunzakuts, 5, 6, 8

-J-

Jerky, alternate name for fruit leather, 37

-K-

Kumquats, drying of, 74

-L-

Leather, fruit and vegetable, 37-48
  ancient preservation method, 37
  doneness test, 38
  flavoring additions to, 41
  general instructions for making, 39-40
  honey instead of sugar, 38
  made from old fruit, 39
  made from juice pulp, 41
  made without a blender, 37
  oven drying of, 38
  recipes for all kinds of, 41-45
  storing of, 29-32
  uses for, 45, 46
Lemon, drying of, 74
  leather, 43
Lime, drying of, 74
  leather, 43
Limon leather, 43
Loganberries, drying of, 73

-M-

Mardikian, George, 37
Measurements, equivalent, 34
Metric tables, 34
Micro-organisms, spoilage caused by, 6-8
Mulberries, drying of, 74
Mushrooms, drying of, 95
  in recipes, 91
Muskmelon, drying of, 74

-N-

Natural sals and sugars, concentrated in
  dried produce, 8
Nectarines, drying of, 76
  in leather, 43
  treated as peaches, 51
Net, nylon, spread on screen, 11-13
  catches drips, 12
  protects against insects, 11
  protects fingernails, 12
  substitute for oven rack, 13

-O-

Okra, drying of, 96
Onions, drying of, 96
  versatility of, 82
Onion powder, 96
Oven drying, 12-15
  advantages of, 15
  disadvantages of, 14, 15
  on screen rack, 13
  on improvised net rack, 13
  precautions and heat regulation, 13, 14
  testing oven, 14

-P-

Papaya, drying of, 76
Pasteurization, 18, 29-30
  of beans, peas, 80
Pea pods, drying of, 96
Peaches, drying of, 76
  leather, 44
  recipes for, 52-61
  uses for, 51
Pears, drying of, 76
  leather, 44
  recipes for, 52-68
  uses for, 51
Peas, drying of, 96
Pectin solution, as pretreatment, 26
Peppers, drying of, 96
Persimmons, drying of, 76
  leather, 45
  uses of, 51
Pineapple, drying of, 77
  leather, 44
  restores color in "old fruit" leather, 39
  uses for, 52
Pineapple juice, as pretreatment, 26
Plastic wrap, used in making leather, 38-39
  garbage can liners, not to be used, 40
Plums, drying of, 77
  leather, 44
  recipes for, 52-68
  uses for, 52
Potatoes, sweet, drying of, 96
Potatoes, white, drying of, 96
  in recipes, 90
  special pretreatment required, 81
Pretreatment of fruits and vegetables, 31-38
  ascorbic acid, 23
  boiling water blanching, 27-28
  "gilding the lily," 28
  honey-lemon juice, 26
  pectin solution, 26
  pineapple juice, 26
  reasons for, 23, 72-78
  salt solution, 25
  steaming, 27-28
  sulfur, 23-25
  sodium bisulfite, 23-24
Prunes, drying of, 77
  leather, same as plum, 44

recipes for, 52-61
uses for, 52
Pumpkin, drying and using, 107, 108, 109

-R-

Raspberries, drying of, 74
  leather, 45
Reconstitution of dried foods, 50
  five minutes in boiling water, 52, 53, 56, 57, 58, 59, 63, 64, 65, 66, 67, 68, 69, 70, 71
Rhubarb, drying of, 77
  leather, 45
  recipes for, 69-71
Room drying, 11, 12
  convenient places, 11
  herbs bunched, 12
  threading food on string, 12
Rutabagas, drying of, 97

-S-

Salt solution as pretreatment, 23
Sodium bisulfite as pretreatment, 23-24
Solar drying, principle and practice of, 18
Spoilage, causes of, 6-8
Squash, drying of, 96
  versatility of, 82
Steaming as pretreatment, 27
Storing dried foods, 29-32
  equalizing moisture, 29
  guidelines for, 30-32
  if too dry, 32
  in freezer, 31
  in glass jars, 31
  in metal cans, 31
  in plastic, 31
  in plastic bags, 31
Sulfuring (outdoor), 24
Sulfurer, sketch of, 24
Sun drying, 15-18
  disadvantages of, 16-18
  on clothesline, 15
  on suspended frame, 16
  on door or window screens, 16
  screened-in dryer, 16-17
Syrup solution as pretreatment, 26

-T-

Tomatoes, drying of, 97

117

Subject Index

in recipes, 83, 90, 92
uses of, 83
Turnips, drying of, 97
TVP, textured vegetable protein, 104

-V-

Vegetables, need for pretreatment, 79
reconstitution of, 81
sensible economy in drying of, 79
test for doneness, 80, 94-97
vine drying of beans and peas, 80

Vitamins, loss of A, C, D, in dried foods, 6, 7

-W-

Watermelon, drying of, 77
uses of, 52

-Z-

Zucchini, drying of, 97
in recipes, 92, 93
uses of, 83